# Journey Through KURDISTAN

TEXT AND PHOTOGRAPHS BY
MARY ANN SMOTHERS BRUNI

TEXAS MEMORIAL MUSEUM
THE UNIVERSITY OF TEXAS AT AUSTIN

Texas Memorial Museum
2400 Trinity
Austin, Texas 78705

The exhibition and publication *Journey through Kurdistan* were
made possible in part by grants from the Texas Committee for the
Humanities, the National Endowment for the Humanities, and the
J. E. Smothers, Sr., Memorial Foundation.

Published in 1995 by Texas Memorial Museum.
Printed in the United States of America.

Library of Congress Catalog Card No. 95-61950

Cover:  Returning to Qala Diza ©1991 Mary Ann Smothers Bruni
Map of Kurdistan: Jonathan Wyss ©1994 TexArt Services
Book Design:  Mary Bean
ISBN 0-941671-00-3
ISBN 0-941671-01-1 (pbk.)

# CONTENTS

# Acknowledgements

My journey was not one I embarked upon alone. I made many friends and met many colleagues along the way, all of whom added to my knowledge and pleasure. Thanks to them and to the varied experiences we shared, I returned, as one should from a journey, with new perspectives on life and the world that will serve me as well in Texas as in Kurdistan.

Mine was a woman's "journey among brave women," to paraphrase the title of the 1964 book about Dana Schmidt's travels in Kurdistan. While Kurds of both sexes offered me the generous hospitality for which they are justifiably famous, I usually was the guest of women and was often passed from hostess to hostess as I made my way through Kurdistan. I remember my Kurdish women friends warmly, cherish their friendship, and admire their courage and tenacity in the face of many hardships. As Gulbihar told her husband Emer of the Golden Hand in the Kurdish epic poem *The Fortress of Dimdim*, Kurdish women and men are equally brave. "The strength of all lions is the same, and it is the lion's blood that runs in both our veins."

In homes and communities Kurdish women encourage and help one another. Through laudable organizations such as *Zhinan*, the Women's Union of Kurdistan, Kurdish women who are able aid their bereaved and tragedy-stricken sisters to get back on their feet and strive to take the story of Kurdish women to the outside world. Among such women who contributed their time, talents, knowledge, and possessions to create this exhibition and book *Journey through Kurdistan* were Hero Talabani, Nazanin Mohammed Rasheed, Kafiya Suleyman, Faima Barzani, Dr. Atia Salihy, Ala Talabani, her cousin Kurdistan, and most especially my very dear friend Leila and her daughter Aisha.

It is said that the knights-errant of medieval Europe based their code of chivalry on the example of civility and bravery set by the valiant leader of their foes, the most famous of all Kurds, Salah al Din al-Ayyubi, known in the West as Saladin, King of Jerusalem. Certainly the *peshmerga* (literally "those who face death") who guarded and guided me throughout Kurdistan embodied the service, loyalty, bravery, and politeness worthy of Kurdish warrior-knights. Gallant Kurdish lances at my service included young men known as Hoyshar, Naryman, Samir, Aziz, Asad, Younis, Hasan, Raoof, Kawa, and Kak Ahmad and his son Samde. Peshmerga who graduated to be Kurdish politicians and leaders were also of great assistance to my travels, particularly Omar and Bekir Fatah, and their mother Aisha Khan, Bekir Haji Safir and his wife Kafiya Khan, Rustum Mohammed ("Mam Rustum") Rahim, Rust Shawals, Pir Khadir Suleyman, Hussein Sanjauri, Hoyshar Zebari, Jamal Aziz, Haquim Qadir, Sami Abdulrakhman, Sheikh Abdullah Barzani, Siamand Bannah, the two Kurdish leaders Jalal Talabani and Massoud Barzani, and Kurdish elder-statesman Ibrahim Ahmad.

The Ali Sheban family of Amadiya, who were my hosts for three months in 1991 and whom I continued to visit throughout my stay in Kurdistan, received me into their home like a member of the family. Mr. Ali, his wife Leila, and their sons and daughters, nieces and nephews were dear to me as few people have been in my life. Their friend Mr. Naji, the retired geography teacher-turned-farmer at Ribar, was a fountain of Kurdish history, customs, and ideas. He, his wife Selwan, their seven children, and his kinswoman Huriya helped make my stay at Amadiya happy and informative.

The Kurdistan that I knew also became home to the allied soldiers who created the Safe-haven in northern Iraq, to the relief workers who made it inhabitable, and to the scholars, journalists, human-rights activists, and photographers who took advantage of the opportunity to visit parts of Kurdistan that had been closed to independent investigators for years. "American peshmerga," as Colonel Richard Naab sometimes called the soldiers of the rescue mission Operation Provide Comfort, often facilitated information and travel for me. I am grateful to Colonel Naab, Colonel Richard Wilson, Colonel Robert Young, who were commanders of the Military Coordination Center at Zakho between 1991 and 1993, General John Shalikashvili, who commanded Operation Provide Comfort from Incirlik, Turkey, in 1991, and most especially, to General Jay Garner, commander of Operation Provide Comfort in northern Iraq in 1991.

The brave doctors, nurses, engineers, and relief workers who helped restore the ravished area were my friends and informants, as well as the heroes of Kurdistan. Interviews with Fred Cuny, singled out by Kurdish leaders as the one relief-worker most responsible for bringing Kurds out of the mountains and establishing them in the Safe-haven, were particularly helpful in comprehending the rescue and subsequent relief effort.

Scholars from the School of Oriental and African Studies (SOAS) at the University of London were on the forefront of investigative studies in Kurdistan and diligently disseminated firsthand knowledge of the area through symposia, publications, lectures, and public discussions. Dr. Philip Kreyenbroek, founder of the Society of Iranian Oral Studies, generously shared his knowledge with me, helped organize the material for my exhibition script and this book, and advised the development of both. Christine Allison made her translations of women's oral literature available to me, and Maria O'Shea kindly read my text and offered many valuable suggestions.

Commentary on the Jews of Kurdistan is based on conversations with Dr. Yona Sabar of the University of California at Los Angeles, with whom I traveled to his home town of Zakho, Iraq, and to visit Kurdish Jews in Israel, and on sections of his book *The Folk Literature of the Kurdistani Jews*. My firsthand impressions of Kurdish rugs were checked against William Eagleton's authoritative *An Introduction to Kurdish Rugs and Other Weavings*; Ambassador Eagleton kindly met with me at SOAS in London and clarified my questions about Kurdish weavers and their response to the difficult circumstances under which they produced. Publications of Middle East Watch and discussions with Joost Hiltermann, project director of their Kurdish investigations, and Andrew Whitely, director of Middle East Watch, confirmed and expanded the stories that I heard about the Anfal operation. The staff of the Library of the School of Oriental and African Studies at the University of London and Dr. Vera Beaudin Saeedpour, director of The Kurdish Library in Brooklyn, New York, provided important support on researching both cultural and political matters and in putting the current situation in historical perspective.

Turkish journalists and politicians examining the tragic conflict between Turks and Kurds provided useful insights into the struggle in their country. Outstanding in their comprehension of the problem were Uluç Gürkan, editor-in-chief of *Sabah* turned parliamentary deputy, and Ragip Duran, who worked with the *Cumhuriyet*, BBC, and the French Agency. Seyfi Tashan, president of the Turkish Institute for Foreign Affairs, meticulously explained the historical development of Turkey's policies to me. Musa Agacik of the *Milliyet* arranged my first visit to Kurdish Turkey in May 1990; former deputy prime minister Erdal İnönü and current deputy prime minister Hikmet Çetin hosted that investigative tour. Ertugrul Gunay, Secretary-General of the People's Republican Party, arranged for me to accompany leaders of that party on their February 1993 examination of the growing tension in the troubled region. Former Turkish first lady Semra Ozal first told me of the problems in southeastern Turkey, where her Foundation for the Elevation and Strengthening of Turkish Women was working, and she was the first person to encourage me to visit the area.

This exhibition and catalogue were made possible by the sponsorship of Texas Memorial Museum, The University of Texas at Austin, the Texas Committee for the Humanities, the National Endowment for the Humanities, and the J. E. Smothers, Sr., Memorial Foundation. Lynn Denton and Jeff Jeffreys of Texas Memorial Museum of The University of Texas, and Mary Bean, Art Director at Sosa, Bromley, Aguilar, Noble and Associates, in San Antonio, Texas, helped edit the photographs for the exhibition and the catalogue, and Dr. Abraham Zilkha and Elizabeth Fernea of The Middle Eastern Center of The University of Texas joined the staff of the museum in editing the text for the exhibition. Many thanks are due Cindy Hughes and Pamela Shepherd, the ever patient and encouraging editors of the text section of this catalogue, and Alice Evett who copy edited and proofread the final text.

My words and images are meant to be but an introduction to the world of the Kurd. I hope that they will encourage readers along their own exploration of the culture of the Kurds and of the problems that plague their region, one which should include reading the books of earlier travelers and those of my colleagues with whom I shared my journey.


Mary Ann Smothers Bruni
San Antonio, Texas

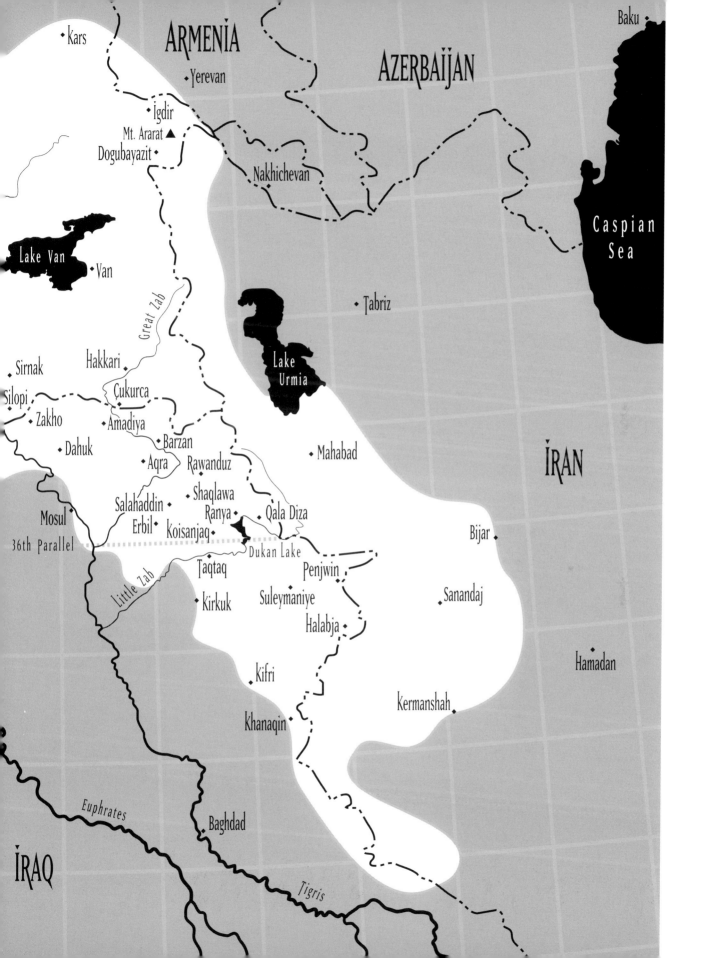

For ***Zhinan***, the brave women of Kurdistan

# FOREWORD

During the year 1991, our nation was engaged in armed conflict with Iraq. This sad culmination led immediately, however, to examination by our citizenry of precipitating events and also to a desire to further understand the cultures of the Middle East, about whose complexities most of us had been very poorly instructed. Information in the press concerning the treatment of the Iraqi Kurdish population by its own government led to expanded appreciation of the Kurds as a complicated group in its own right, whose geographic distribution, generally called Kurdistan, includes significant parts of five countries—Iraq, Iran, Turkey, Syria, and Armenia.

With great interest, therefore, we at the Texas Memorial Museum learned of the repeated travels of Mary Ann Smothers Bruni through parts of Turkey and Iraq from 1990 through 1993, photographing the Kurdish people and recording her impressions of their day-to-day life under varying conditions of civil war, trade embargoes, and United Nations political involvement. From the photographic results of these trips, Ms. Bruni selected the images that form the substance of the exhibition *Journey through Kurdistan* at the Texas Memorial Museum and also provide the heart of this book. Interpretive labeling of the exhibit and text of this volume reflect Ms. Bruni's views of conditions within this part of Kurdistan.

In this sponsorship, the staff of Texas Memorial Museum take pride in adding, in a small way, to understanding of the character and plight of the Kurdish people.

William G. Reeder
Director
Texas Memorial Museum

# İNTRODUCTİON

Kurdistan, "land of the Kurds," is not, and has never been, a country. It is, simply put, "where the Kurds live," a crescent-shaped territory about the size of Texas where the approximately twenty-six million people who call themselves Kurds predominate. The area has also been home to Armenian, Christian Assyrian, Jewish, and Turkoman communities, which in varying degrees feel akin to the Kurds and in a broad sense are part of the Kurdish mountain culture. The land known as Kurdistan is, in fact, a lively patchwork of diverse people and cultures.

The heart of Kurdistan lies high in the Zagros Mountains where the modern countries of Turkey, Iran, and Iraq come together, and it extends into Syria and Armenia. The Zagros and the eastern Taurus Mountains, stretching from northwest to southeast, form the region's backbone. The high mountain ranges that distinguish Kurdistan lie parallel to each other, northwest to southeast. Beginning with the foothills near the Tigris River, each range rises higher than the last until they reach the elevated Persian plateau. Long, narrow valleys separate the ranges, through which rivers flow, cutting magnificent gorges to join the Tigris. To the north the Anatolian highlands border gigantic Lake Van, and beyond lies Mount Ararat, where Biblical tradition says Noah's ark landed.

The mountain ranges, impassable much of the winter, protect the Kurds from their hostile neighbors, as well as separate them from each other. The protection and isolation offered by these mountains have shaped the character and history of the Kurds and are part of what has made them different from their Arab, Turkish, and Persian brothers of the surrounding plains civilizations. Over the centuries the Kurdish mountains have allowed their inhabitants to preserve their traditions and have given refuge to peoples who were persecuted elsewhere. As a proverb says, "Take away their mountains, and you destroy the Kurds."

About 2,500 years ago, the Persians and the Medes created empires that included Kurdistan. Xenophon described the area in the *Anabasis* (401-400 B. C.) and characterized the Carduchi, possible predecessors of the Kurds who lived there, as an independent and feisty people, much the same as nineteenth and twentieth century European travellers later depicted the Kurds. In the mid–seventh century A.D. the Arabs conquered the Kurdish region and began to convert its inhabitants to Islam. In the case of the Kurds, this seems to have been a gradual process, but eventually Islam became the dominant faith in Kurdistan. Unlike many Muslim peoples in the Middle East who soon adopted Arabic, the Kurds continued to speak their own language and were recognized as a distinct people even though they were usually part of much larger states, such as the Turkish Ottoman and the Persian Safivid empires. The photographs and text in this catalogue depict the Kurdish areas of southeastern Turkey and northern Iraq that belonged to the Kurdish emirates of the Bhotan, the Badinan, the Baban, and the Soran during the time they were ruled by the Ottoman Empire.

The Ottoman Empire, an important power from the mid–fifteenth century until World War I, was a multi-national empire in which Turks, Arabs, Greeks, Armenians, Jews, Circassians, Serbs, Croats, Kurds, and others lived their lives, practiced their religions, and spoke their own languages with little interference from the Sublime Porte, as the sultan's government in Istanbul was called. The Ottoman sultan was the religious head of Islam, but "people of the book," which included Christians and Jews, were allowed every privilege in his realm.

When the empire collapsed after World War I, the Western allies sought to divide Ottoman lands into nation-states, or Western-style countries, along ethnic lines, giving the Arabs, Turks, Greeks, Armenians, and Kurds their own states. The 1921 Treaty of Sèvres provided for the creation of a country called Kurdistan. The subsequent Treaty of Lausanne, however, perhaps influenced by the discovery of oil in the Vilayet of Mosul, gave those Kurdish lands, later northern Iraq, to the British, and the Bhotan to the new Republic of Turkey. The only major ethnic group of the former Ottoman Empire denied their own nation-state, the approximately twenty-six million Kurds were condemned to be minorities in the newly formed states. The Kurds became the largest nation in the world without a country.

The leader of Turkey, Mustafa Kemal, known as "Ataturk," father of Turkey, influenced by the nation-state philosophy prevalent in Europe at that time, decided that minorities had burdened and ultimately destroyed the Ottoman Empire. He declared the Kurds in his country to be Turks and ordered them to speak Turkish. Thus began a long period of unrest between Turks and Kurds, which included bloody civil uprisings. Hostilities reached the point where speaking the Kurdish language was outlawed and the very existence of Kurds officially denied by the Turkish government. They became known as "mountain Turks," Turks who in the isolation of their mountain-homes had forgotten their own language.

In March of 1990, tens of thousands of Turkish Kurds living in the towns of Diyarbakir, Silopi, Nuysaybin, and Cizre took to the streets, tearing Turkish flags and crying, *"Biji Kurdistan!* Long live Kurdistan!" They were frustrated by the ever-growing violence and economic disruption caused by continued fighting between Turkish soldiers and the guerrillas of the militant Kurdistan Workers' Party (PKK). Turkish president Turgut Ozal responded with controversial Decree 413, which allowed the forced evacuations of villages, the removal of disruptive people from the Kurdish area to other parts of Turkey, and for the imprisonment of journalists, the closing of print houses, and the fining of publications that produced "incorrect" materials about the situation in southeastern Turkey. What the European press called "Turkey's dirty miniwar," a particularly cruel civil disturbance between Kurds and Turks, has grown progressively more violent from that day to this.

The Kurds enjoyed some cultural freedom and political rights when Great Britain ruled what is now Iraq. The situation grew more difficult under Arab rule, and following a dispute over the terms of the establishment of an autonomous Kurdish zone in the 1970's, ferocious fighting broke out between Kurds and the central government. When the 1974 Treaty of Algiers ended a conflict with the Shah of Iran, the Iraqi government turned on the Kurds, some of whom had sided with the Iranians, and began to demolish their villages, relocate the inhabitants to southern Iraq and government-supervised collective villages, and repopulate strategic areas, such as the oil-rich region of Kirkuk, with Arabs. Conditions grew steadily worse, and following the end of the Iraqi-Iranian war in the 1980's, Saddam Hussein unleashed the 1988 Al-Anfal "spoils of battle" operation against the Kurds. The Anfal included looting, rape, murder, and chemical weapon attacks against Kurdish civilians.

The Persian Gulf War dramatically altered the Kurds' circumstances. Under President Ozal's guidance and perhaps persuaded by pressure from Western allies, Turkey recognized the existence of Kurds and allowed them to speak their language, although the bloody conflict there continued. Encouraged by Saddam's defeat, the Iraqi Kurds took radio messages by American President George Bush for a call to arms. In March 1991, the Iraqi Kurds rose up against Saddam's government and suffered disastrous consequences. It is here that our story begins.

# 1
# KURDISH EXODUS

April 1991

"Food is no. Water is no. Only death is yes." The merciless rain, the children crying, the stench of the dead and the dying accentuated the words of the Kurdish refugee. Rain ran down his tired face as he spoke. Dysentery and cold were finishing off the devastation of the Kurds and other minorities of northern Iraq begun by the regime of Saddam Hussein.

The Kurdish uprising had failed. The Western help that Kurds had anticipated never came. Peshmerga, Kurdish guerrilla fighters (literally "those who face death"), held the lines while terrified civilians, remembering Saddam's 1988 chemical attacks against the Kurds, scrambled to the borders of Turkey and Iran. Not having the resources to accommodate a massive influx of people and worried about political activities of the Kurdish minority in their own country, Turks stopped the refugees at the border with troops.

"Don't go to the camp today," a Turkish soldier warned me on my trek up the mountain from the small town of Çukurca. "The riots are awful. People are fighting over loaves of bread. Can you imagine? It is dangerous for you to be there. Come stand on this ridge with us and photograph with your telephoto lens."

I promised to come back if I had any trouble, but if this were to be the demise of the Iraqi Kurds, caught between ferocious Iraqi air bombardments and diligent Turkish soldiers, it was important to me that I witness it if I must, assist them if I could.

I had first met Iraqi Kurds during the Persian Gulf War, January 1991, in Diyarbakir, Turkey, the temporary home of many of the eighty thousand or so who lived there as "visitors" after fleeing Iraq following chemical attacks against the Kurds in 1988. Their leader had predicted the Kurdish uprising against the government of Saddam and a bright future in a transformed Iraq that would provide freedom and democracy for Kurd, Turkoman, Christian, Shi'ite and Sunni Arab alike. That future looked dismal now.

After a thirty-minute walk up the mountain, I arrived at an open plain of several square miles before the mountains continued upwards. What usually would be described as a magnificent vista was cluttered with close to a hundred thousand people, some with army-type tents, but most sheltered from a light but constant rain beneath makeshift shelters of blankets and plastic coverings. Many had no shelter at all. Officials and information agencies gave wildly varying figures on the numbers of refugees at this and similar camps along the Turkish-Iraqi border, but the constant influx and movement made any such count unreliable.

From the ridge above, the Kurds seemed like milling human ants trapped in some nightmare fashioned by Kafka. They covered the plain and the mountains beyond as far as the eye could see. A bit closer, detail and color became defined and the bright fabrics highlighted with sequins worn by Kurdish village women caught my eye. Slowly, the masses became shopkeepers and schoolteachers, farmers and herders, lawyers and Assyrian Christian priests. One after another, people approached. "Many children lost their shoes in the mud," one man said. "Then the cold came, and the poor children were walking barefoot in the snow."

"Our old people are falling over dead from exhaustion," said another.

"We are not always like this," Abdullah, a thirty-year-old electrical engineer, apologized. His gray slacks and white shirt were amazingly clean given the squalor of the camp. "This is a terrible disaster. We are killed by mines and by cold. There is no clean water. Some of us have money, but we are not allowed to buy or sell at the market in Çukurca. Food distribution is a catastrophe. Trucks toss bread over the side, and everyone scrambles for it. I would buy bread, but people of my status cannot fight villagers for food."

Abdullah introduced me to Nizan, a girl about nine years old, who confided that she wanted a tent more than anything else in the world. "The rain is so cold. My family has no shelter, and the children are getting sick." Almost in answer to her prayer, American military airplanes arrived and began to circle the camp, high above the Kurds at first, then descending ever closer. People looked upwards in awe and expectation. American Secretary of State James Baker had visited the camp for a few minutes two days before, and Kurds were anxious to know what America's reaction would be to their terrible plight.

Something small seemed to fall from the plane, minute bundles that blossomed into colorful parachutes. Against the ominous gray sky, the bright parachutes seemed gifts from another world. As they approached the ground, Kurds could see tents and other supplies attached to them. Whoops of happiness and hope resounded throughout the camp.

We joined Kurds running toward the parachutes. Suddenly one of the glorious blossoms high in the sky wilted into nothing and fell straight down right in front of us, crushing a young girl to death. People nearby shrieked; Nizan grabbed my hand and squeezed hard, then buried her head in my jacket. "She knew Awara, the girl who was killed. Their families are friends," Abdullah explained. Awara's father had been killed and her mother lost during the long walk from Dahuk. The sixteen-year-old girl left two younger sisters, ages eight and six. Fortunately, they had aunts in the camp. Abdullah walked over to a nearby tent crowded with women and children; he leaned down and spoke with one of the women. Already numb with pain, she only grimaced. When she told the two young girls what had happened, they screamed, then began to sob hard and tear their hair.

Stunned by the afternoon's events, I accepted an invitation from Abdullah to spend the night in his cousin Sherko's tent. The trying day, photographing first hope, then death, in the ice-cold rain, was followed by a magical evening of warm Kurdish hospitality, teaching me something of the quick transition Kurds make between tragedy and celebration. We were three men, two wives, five children, a baby, and myself—a cozy number for the tent. The candlelit smiles of the women and the striking profiles of the men were worthy of heroes and heroines in a medieval epic. Their quiet dignity lent elegance to our humble tent set in the most terrible of circumstances.

The men, who spoke English, were anxious to tell their story and share their dinner of goat cheese flavored with pungent Kurdish herbs, scrambled eggs, and bread. "This is the last of our food from home. Enjoy it with us, please," Sherko urged. Knowing too well how precious food was, I took only a few bites from the common dish and had a welcome sip of tea.

The son of an Arab sheikh and a Kurdish mother, Abdullah had been schooled in London from age sixteen through university. In 1987 he moved to Kuwait to work. "First Saddam ruined Kuwait for me, then my own home country. Over a hundred thousand Iraqis, Kurds and Arabs alike, have been killed by this madness. Who will care for the orphans, the old people?" he asked. "Sherko's wife is too starved to give milk for her baby boy. She walks two miles to get safe water for the boy, who lives mostly on sugar water. What might now happen to him? We are like animals here. I am a sheikh's son, an engineer. I have a beautiful girlfriend in California who studied with me in London. I would rather go home and die than live like this."

Sherko wore traditional Kurdish dress. With his scarf and pronounced Kurdish features, complemented by the tent and candlelight, he looked a bit like the star of a twenties' desert movie. "My wife cried the entire trip," he told me. "She came with my family; her family went another way. I was a teacher. Now what can I do to help my family?"

"My wife and I were married four months ago," the third cousin, Mustafa, confided. "This has not been a pleasant wedding trip for her, I fear," he tried to joke.

"We hope when our tragedy is over, when we return to our homes, that you will visit us in Kurdistan, climb our mountains and sit by our waterfalls, eat our tasty fruit and drink our sweet water," Sherko said. "Kurdistan is still beautiful, even though Saddam has ravished it and we now must all carry guns."

Sherko and his family were from Dahuk, the administrative capital of an Iraqi province by the same name. Kurds still called that region the Badinan, after the Kurdish emirate to which it had belonged. The Badinan was the most traditional part of Kurdistan; it was a fertile land blessed with springs and good for raising grain and grazing sheep. For all the pain they had suffered during their flight, the men smiled as they talked of their homeland.

A visitor entered the tent and spoke softly to Sherko. They both left suddenly. "He told Sherko that his niece just died and asked him to bury her," Abdullah told me. As we settled to sleep, toe to toe, we almost filled the tent. The rain continued steadily all throughout the night.

The next morning, I visited other tents and shelters. "Better Saddam had killed us," an older man echoed the sentiments of many in the camp. "Here we watch our children die, one by one." The day grew wetter and more people arrived at the camp. By evening, we were twice as many in our tent. We ate camp relief rice and slept cramped, piled on top of one another. People continued to arrive at the tent throughout the night. The rain, the coughing of the adults, and the crying of the baby and a child were constant. At first light I stepped outside. It seemed that children were crying and old people were coughing in every tent. The voices of tens of thousands of children cried out in unison for help to Allah himself.

That afternoon I met the very elegant Musa, a petroleum engineer. Standing outside his tent in British tweeds, he appeared to be an English country squire. "I am not political or a Kurd. I worked with the government. In two weeks' time, the brave Kurds took our province of Dahuk. They had the courage and weapons to defend themselves, but they could not fight the helicopters. When Saddam began bombarding Dahuk with artillery, I had no choice but to escape in my car with my family. When we ran out of gas, we had to abandon the car and all our goods and walk.

"I saw tens of children die before my very eyes. Before my very eyes, I saw old people drop dead. It didn't seem real; it was like something you see on the television. Seven days wandering through the mountains. I cannot walk now. General Schwarzkopf was right: You should have gone on to Baghdad. Saddam has devastated Kuwait. He is devastating Iraq. He is the number one dictator of all the world. If allowed, he will hit another country. Over two million people are homeless and wandering in northern Iraq now.

"The Kurdish uprising would not have happened if Bush himself had not called on the people of Iraq to revolt. I myself heard him on the radio. 'It is your country, your game, get up and play it,' his propaganda said. Now Saddam the devastator is still in power, but the people of Iraq are displaced and dying. Someone must help immediately, without committees, without meetings, or we shall all be dead."

Musa's family and tent managed to be charming. His wife, mother-in-law, and daughters sat erect, dressed in beautiful caftans, their hair gracefully covered by flowing scarves. His wife, who spoke educated English, had managed to bring spices and homemade pickles with her to create a delicious rice. "Saddam and Bush are one to me," she told me. "It is terrible what they have done to my family."

When my driver arrived and I bade farewell to my friends, a man clad in the traditional dress of the peshmerga threw himself at my feet. "Take this message back. Haji Bush: We pray for you. We kiss your hand. Please finish this man Saddam. Please make it safe for us to go to our homes in peace."

# 2
# AMADÌYA

May 1991

The allied armies brought the Kurds down out of the mountains and secured a Safe-haven for them in northern Iraq. The area above the thirty-sixth parallel was proclaimed a no-fly zone for Iraqi aircraft; allied troops were stationed in the area to protect the Kurds, and food and medicine were being supplied by the U.S. Army and disaster agencies. The "Humanitarians From Hell," led by American Colonels Jim Jones and Steve Epstein, were helping to clean out water supplies, build latrines, and do whatever was necessary. The relief effort, which had the code name of Operation Provide Comfort, was run out of Incirlik Air Force Base in Adana, Turkey, by American Lieutenant General John Shalikashvili and headed in northern Iraq by Major General Jay Garner.

In late May, after a trip home to recover from a bad infection contracted in the mountains with the Kurds, I entered the Safe-haven from Turkey and set out with a car and driver to find my friend Sherko and his family, whose suffering I had shared in Çukurca. Following a brief visit with American officials in Zakho, ten miles from the Turkish border, I headed thirty miles south to Dahuk, a small city of white buildings baking in the summer heat. Houses were missing like teeth from an old man; Saddam had knocked them out with heavy artillery. On a jeep tour through the city, I searched for my friends and rattled off their names to turbaned men sitting in a restaurant. They knew none of them, but sent me to the office of a doctor who had been at Çukurca. He was seated in a hot, dusty walkup office, a photograph of Saddam prominent on the wall behind his desk.

"That was from before," he assured me. Before Kuwait? Before the uprising? The photograph was still there. He turned out to be the brother of my Çukurca friend Musa, who had since moved to Baghdad. "There is no law and order left in Dahuk. The anarchy here is frightening. Anyone could be killed," he warned. He left no doubt that he, too, soon would be out of here. Dahuk was hot, dusty, and chaotic. It was not the idyllic land of Kurdistan described by my friends in their tent at Çukurca, the land blessed with mountains and waterfalls, tasty fruit and sweet water. I wanted to find the Kurdistan that they had described.

Throwing my fate to the wind, I blindly instructed my driver, "Take this road." Up, we drove. Up and up into the famed mountains of Kurdistan. As we ascended, the air became thinner and finer, the light softer, as if filtered through silk chiffon. Whenever we rose to the heights of one range, others beckoned. Ridge after ridge rippled like waves at sea, as we wound ever upward. Around one bend, Amadiya, the ancient capital of the Kurdish emirate of the Badinan, rose suddenly, surely out of the mist, a small fortress city set atop a plateau in the mountains, looking very much like picture-book depictions of Camelot.

Just before the road turned towards Amadiya, a handsome young man clad in the baggy pants of the peshmerga, with a Kalashnikov Russian attack rifle in hand, sat in front of a waterfall, a visual representation of both the natural beauty and the underlying violence that are part of Kurdistan. Below him was an open-air tea house filled with men wearing baggy trousers, colorful cummer-bunds, and shoes with turned-up toes. This was Sulaf, a former resort just below Amadiya. We got out to photograph and have tea. A passing helicopter added its rhythm to the men's chatter.

As the sun waned and dusk approached, my driver suggested a drive back to Dahuk. But the rhythm of the tea chat and the majesty of the mountains had mesmerized me. This was the Kurdistan of which my friends had spoken. I would stay here. I remembered a hotel up the road and had my driver take me there.

Around the bend and up, less than a minute away, toward Dahuk, the Sulaf Hotel stood almost majestically on its own plateau, slightly below Amadiya. A peshmerga with a Kalashnikov greeted us. "This is a peshmerga hotel," my driver translated. "There are no women here."

But I saw a woman walking down the side of the hotel. "There is a woman," I pointed her out.

"But she is the wife of our commander."

"Ask if I can stay with her," I persisted.

The peshmerga obeyed. Apparently she said yes, for our car was beset by a small army of peshmerga. They gathered my luggage and cameras and marched into the hotel. I followed. Up the steps, through a spacious lobby with marble floors and substantial leather and wood chairs, down a flight of stairs, through an aluminum frame that once held a glass door, down a hallway over torn carpet to a war-worn corner suite that would be my apartment for the summer.

The small entrance room with a sofa would serve my driver, and the larger room with two beds, a dresser, a closet, and a bath would be mine. The carpet and drapes were torn, the furniture battered. Through another aluminum frame with no glass, a patio offered a small mulberry tree and a magnificent view of Amadiya. Was it from this amazing hotel that Kurdish warriors had sallied forth to meet their foes? And who was my mysterious hostess?

I walked back up the stairs and out onto a large parking lot, where I encountered a pleasant blond man in European-style clothes. "Welcome to Kurdistan," he said, offering his hand. "I am Asmat. We are happy to have you and most grateful for the help Americans are giving us."

I introduced myself.

"Are you a journalist? We need writers to tell our story to the world immediately."

"Everyone knows your tragedy now, but they will forget you when it is over. I should like to stay here for a while and come to know the Kurds better, how you live when you are not trapped on the side of a mountain, your day-to-day chores, concerns, and passions, and create a document that will reflect the courage and warmth I knew at Çukurca, something that will be here when the front-page stories are gone."

"Please be our guest for as long as you like."

"I seem to have a hostess here," I told him. "Who is she?"

"You are most fortunate," Asmat said with a broad smile. "Leila Khan is the Jacqueline Kennedy of Amadiya."

As there was no electricity in Amadiya, I settled into my room as dusk turned into night. No sooner had I put on my nightclothes and sat on my bed than a lamp appeared, attached to two phantom ladies in flowing gowns. One wore a gossamer multi-hued dress typical of Kurdish villagers and the other a long, straight pink cotton dress adorned with embroidery and a large white scarf.

"Madame, good evening. How are you? Are you well?" asked the young woman with the scarf. They sat on the bed. "Welcome to Kurdistan. We hope your trip was pleasant. I am Aisha. This is my brother's wife Tureen. Will you join us for dinner? Our mother would like to meet you."

We walked down the hall to the next corner suite. It had a large living area, the size of my entire quarters. I sat on a sofa. Their mother sat to my left. "This is our mother, Leila, Madame. She welcomes you and asks you to excuse the conditions of our home. This is our life these days."

Leila, a small, plump woman with an abundant cascade of black hair, dressed in a flowing Kurdish gown, grabbed my hand and smiled. "*Kurdistan xosh e?*" she asked me cheerfully.

"Do you think Kurdistan is nice, Madame? Mother would like to know," Aisha asked.

"Kurdistan is very nice."

"*Kurdistan gelek xosh e,*" smiled Leila.

"*Kurdistan gelek xosh e,*" I parroted. "You are my friend and Kurdish teacher. Thank you very much."

"*Gelek sipas.* Thank you very much," Leila laughed and squeezed my hand.

The light of the lanterns and the patterns of shadows cast by the flowing gowns of the young women lent the room an air of romance. A young peshmerga with a tray of food appeared and served a simple meal of rice and vegetables. "Eat, Madame," invited Aisha. "Mother says she is sorry for the room and the food, but in these circumstances, what can we do?"

"The food and the room are lovely, *gelek xosh e.*"

Leila laughed again.

Twenty-six-year-old Aisha had a business degree from the University of Mosul, where she had learned English. Her father was Ali Sheban, a brave and powerful *agha*, one of the leaders of the uprising. The family was from Amadiya, but until the uprising they had lived in Dahuk and in Baghdad.

"My driver?" I asked.

"Don't worry, Madame," said Aisha. "We have sent him something to eat."

After dinner Aisha gave me a clay bottle of cool water to take to my room. "For you, Madame. We fetch it fresh from the spring every night. Let us know if you need anything."

Life with Leila, her daughters, and her grandchildren was very pleasant. Leila would hold my hand and teach me Kurdish phrases. "*Xisco men i*" she would say. "You are my sister." Since the young male cousins called her Leila Khan, I began to do the same. "*Maria Khan,*" she laughed. "Khan" it turned out, was a peculiarly Kurdish abbreviation for *khanum*, a title like "Lady."

Leila's ten-year-old grandson Ari taught me to count in Kurdish. "*Yek, doo, sey, char, penj.*" We practiced in the afternoons. Habiba, one of Leila's daughters, tried my makeup and modeled handsome family gold jewelry for me, including a wide belt that dragged the floor. Aisha translated lively conversations with her sisters and sister-in-law, young ladies almost the same ages as my four daughters; they became my Kurdish children. We exchanged ideas about makeup, clothes, and, of course, men.

"Madame, we have heard that in America women have their freedom at eighteen. What does that mean?" Aisha asked anxiously.

"It means they are free to leave home if they like, Aisha. Another freedom they have is to go out with young men and choose their own husband. Would you like to do that?"

"*Why*, Madame? Father can make very good matches for us."

And what did Kurdish girls most want in husbands? "A good husband should be rich and powerful and intelligent . . . oh, yes, and very handsome."

A young woman could refuse her father's choice if she was not "comfortable" with him. Were Aisha's sisters Habiba and Jihan "comfortable" with their husbands?

"Oh, yes, Madame," giggled Aisha, "my sisters are both *very* comfortable with their husbands."

Marriage in Kurdistan was often between first cousins who had known each other since childhood. The favored choice was a father's brother's child. Or a young person might marry an equal from another family, usually to bond the families. Jihan had married within the family, while Habiba had married a man from another wealthy, powerful family.

Leila replaced my driver with her young nephew Halit. While male family members and Haji, who had been raised with Mr. Ali and served as a personal guard, could enter into Leila's domain, it was forbidden to other males. Unwittingly, I had moved into a Kurdish agha's harem. The word "harem" means "forbidden" and has nothing to do with lascivious goings-on. A *haremlik* is a women's section of a house forbidden to men, an Ottoman arrangement that denotes protection and status. Keeping women separate is a very expensive task, not at all practical for ordinary households.

At first, I rarely saw Leila's husband, Mr. Ali, although he lived in the hotel. If he were in Leila's apartment when I entered, he immediately left. Mr. Ali was wiry and spry. He moved like an athlete and cut quite a handsome figure in the classical Badinan suits of dark blue or stripes that he usually wore, complete with turban, cummerbund, and shoes with turned-up toes. A British friend of mine thought he resembled Yul Brynner. Mr. Ali had been a *mustashar*, a commander of Saddam's Kurdish militia, who switched to the rebel side during the uprising. Mr. Ali's reputation as a fighting man was such that Iraqi troops in the area surrendered their guns without a fight or joined the Kurdish forces. Amadiya went over to the Kurds without a battle. After the rebellion collapsed, Mr. Ali enhanced his reputation as a courageous warrior when he and his troops held the Iraqi forces at Zawita, a resort not far from Amadiya, while civilians fled to Turkey. Mr. Ali had fought bravely until wounded and taken to Iran, at which time his men joined their families in the massive flight.

After about a week, Mr. Ali recognized that Leila, the girls, and I had become special friends and began to treat me as a female member of the family. He and Leila were cordial, generous, and protective, always making certain that I was well attended when I left the hotel and graciously received wherever I went. The powerful agha and fighting man was a loving husband and father and a particularly doting grandfather, always carrying his two-year-old grandson Mohammed in his arms, laughing and talking to him. He teased his daughter Habiba about having cut the child's hair very short like that of the allied soldiers. "Father says that everyone is going to think that Mohammed is the son of an American soldier," Aisha would raise her eyebrow and giggle.

About two weeks after I arrived, Leila decided to declare a late observance of Ramadan, the Islamic month of fasting and prayer. Muslims have the option of carrying out the fast at a later date if they are unable to do so at the proper time. This year, the Kurds had not been able to observe Ramadan correctly because of the exodus. Muslims would read the Qu'ran and visit mosques and holy shrines during Ramadan. Every day of Ramadan was sort of a combination of Good Friday and Mardi Gras. During that time, a Muslim could not eat or drink even water, smoke, or have sexual relations from first light until dark. Families and friends would get together at night, however, for fun and food, then sleep very little before awakening early to enjoy a large breakfast together before light returned.

The girls added prayers and Qu'ran reading to their daytime activities. Leila, who preferred the social aspects of Ramadan, slept during the day. Nights we donned our *abas*, black cotton cloaks, and had the young peshmerga drive us up to Amadiya to the house of Leila's sister. In the happy seclusion of her garden, we picnicked, a favorite Kurdish pastime, until the wee hours of the morning. Both generations of sisters gossiped and laughed, clearly delighting in one another's company. Kurdish women, like many women in the Middle East, are very affectionate with one another. While men and women never touch in public, women constantly hold hands and embrace.

Once electricity had been restored, we made occasional nighttime visits to a friend who lived in a house up the hill from the tea house by the falls. With electricity back, the tea house became a lively evening gathering place for the area men. We would spread a blanket outside, sip tea, and watch the comings and goings below. But my friend Leila never showed any desire to be a part of that male world; just as Mr. Ali had his friends and his political realm, Leila had hers.

My friendship with Leila became such that a Turkish friend teased me, "She is going to want to make you Ali's second wife so that you can stay together."

That, of course, never happened. One day, however, Aisha approached me with an interesting proposition. "Madame, Mother says if you have no husband, she can arrange for you to marry a very rich and very wise and very handsome Kurdish man. Then you can stay here and always be her good friend." I was certain that Leila was willing and able to do exactly that. While having to turn down the touching and generous offer, I let Aisha know how very pleased and flattered I was to be considered such a close part of the family.

Being from the West, I could also be invited upstairs to meet Mr. Ali's guests. Friends who visited the Sulaf while I was there included Kurdish leaders, holy men, and tribal chiefs, as well as a healthy assortment of foreign dignitaries. Jalal Talabani, the founder and leader of the Patriotic Union of Kurdistan, or the PUK, came for breakfast one morning with one hundred twenty-five of his personal guard; the Assyrian Christian Bishop of Dahuk came the next afternoon for tea. Rather than feeling any envy, the women were delighted by my upstairs privileges, which provided them with a firsthand source for gossip about Kurdistan's rich and famous.

Huriya, a family member from Amadiya, had lost almost everything in the uprising, including her husband, two houses, her furniture, and most of her clothes. Nevertheless, she insisted on giving me one of her dresses to wear, a long flowing gown of blue lace, and a black sequined coat to go over it. The Badinan dresses are long and loose with elastic at the waist. The sleeves are snug to the wrist, then fall dramatically to the floor. When the sleeves are not tied, the dresses look like those worn by Guinivere and her entourage at King Arthur's court. Most often the dresses are covered by a full floor-length coat also with long sleeves. The sleeves of the dress are pulled through those of the coat and wound around the wearer's arm, or tied together in front and thrown over her back, slightly restraining the woman and making her movements more stately. These gowns are worn all day, for cleaning, cooking, climbing to the springs, or picking mulberries. In most homes, which do not have separate sleeping quarters as our hotel did, the gowns are also worn for sleeping.

Huriya liked to go to Ribar, a small community in the narrow valley between Amadiya and Sulaf, to lunch with Mr. Naji, a retired history teacher; his wife, Selwan; their seven daughters, all named for flowers; and his two sons, named for his favorite heroes, Mohammed and Richard the Lion-Hearted. But wasn't Richard the enemy of that most famous of Kurds, Salah al Din al-Ayyubi, known to the West as Saladin, King of Jerusalem? Perhaps, Mr. Naji would say, but he was brave and good and a poet, all that a man should be.

Mr. Naji loved to talk about Kurdistan. Legend says that the Kurds descend from five hundred *jinn,* spirits, exiled from the Kingdom of Solomon and five hundred European virgins that they abducted and brought with them to their new home in the Zagros Mountains. According to tradition, the Kurds are descendants of the ancient Medes and had lived in these mountains for thousands of years before the Turks or Arabs arrived. "A people with such a long history deserve to have a government," Mr. Naji would say. The facts surrounding the Persian Gulf War baffled him. He could not comprehend why a million Kuwaitis had a country while twenty-six million Kurds did not. Nor could he understand why the West had gone to war in 1991 to save the Kuwaitis and their independence, yet had supported Saddam in 1988 while he burnt Kurdish villages and inflicted terrible chemical punishment upon the Kurdish people. Now that it appeared that the allied troops would be pulling out of northern Iraq, Mr. Naji, like most of the Kurds, was apprehensive about what Saddam's next move against the Kurds might be.

One day Aisha told me that her father had requested that I have tea with him upstairs. His nephew Asmat would translate. Mr. Ali, Asmat, and I sat upstairs by a large window overlooking Amadiya. I thanked Mr. Ali for the generous hospitality that his family had offered me. "This is our duty, to extend all kindness and assistance because you have come to fulfill a humanitarian mission to the Kurdish people. The Kurds are not happy, not comfortable now. Like most Iraqi citizens, we wish that the allies would put more pressure on Saddam Hussein so that he would have to end this torture."

Mr. Ali's assessment of the Kurds' future was bleak. He had no faith that an agreement with Saddam would be reached. While very appreciative of America's humanitarian aid, he could not comprehend our leaving Saddam to rule, which he likened to leaving Hitler in Germany. He worried about the economic collapse of Iraq, which had left the men of the Kurdish area with no work, no duties, no business. "Everyone is waiting," he said. "No one can invest money in such a place. I fear we will lose everything."

During the fighting Mr. Ali and his family had lost three cars, more than thirty Persian carpets, two households of silver and antiques, and most of their clothes. He was worried about the rumored American pullout from Kurdistan and asked if I knew the American officials here or had any information.

Mr. Ali had another problem. Besides the family at Sulaf, he had a second wife, Pani, and children in Baghdad, and was worried about their safety and well-being. He very much feared that all of his family would be killed by assassins in the hire of Saddam and the incident blamed on old rivalries between Kurds. Mr. Ali wanted me to meet Pani and his other children. When I asked if she got along with Leila, Mr. Ali clasped his forehead and closed his eyes as if in intense pain. He had to keep them in different cities, he admitted. I thanked him, but I loved Leila and her children and did not wish to betray them.

Hoyshar, a very large and amiable young bodyguard of Jalal Talabani, who stayed upstairs at the hotel when his leader traveled abroad, introduced me to local peshmerga. He would take me to the peshmerga camp in the nearby mountains, where we would share lunch with the men in the shade of a large oak tree. "Peshmerga must always be polite and correct, as well as brave," the commander there would tell me. "It is our duty to be hospitable to visitors and loyal to Kurdistan." The code of honor of these knights-errant in baggy pants was strict and demanding. Young peshmerga would often fulfill their obligations to serve Kurdistan by assisting visitors. Hoyshar became the first of many young peshmerga who would quite happily serve as my guides, translators, and guards during my next two years of travels in Kurdistan.

One day Hoyshar brought me an invitation to a peshmerga art exhibition in Dahuk, which he insisted I attend. It also was a pretext to gather for a march on "Hotel Dahuk," the allied base. The Kurds carried signs reading, "Finish what you have started" and, to my great delight, "Americans please don't go home." They joined almost everyone in the Badinan in lamenting the coming pullout of the Americans. Major General Jay Garner, our man in Iraq, came down to talk with the demonstrators. He shook hands with many of the peshmerga and explained to the crowd that the allies were not leaving Iraq right away, but simply moving their headquarters to Zakho, near the Turkish border, and some of their troops to Silopi, Turkey.

"Hey, Mary Ann!" he hollered when he saw me. I was surprised that he remembered me from our brief conversation in Zakho. The allied leaders, however, may have been as interested in what my friends and I were doing in Amadiya as we were in what they were doing in Dahuk. He asked me in to chat, then invited me to join him the next morning in a helicopter flight over the Safe-haven. I grabbed my gear from the car and shared the allied soldiers' last night at Hotel Dahuk, enjoying a good American-style meal and listening to the guys reminisce about the rescue operation here. One described it as "the experience of a lifetime," another as "the most fun I've ever had." All agreed that helping so many people had given them a sense of satisfaction that one rarely knows. General Garner was quite fond of teasing the "disaster groupies," as he called the professional rescue workers, but he readily admitted that the success of Operation Provide Comfort had made him consider joining the Peace Corps when he retired. "Rescue and relief work would be a good use of the talents of retired generals and colonels," he said.

Disaster worker Fred Cuny, greatly admired by the Kurds as the ultimate American can-do man, was there. Cuny had won high marks from the Kurds for successfully negotiating this year's harvest. In an attempt to Arabize the area, Saddam had given Kurdish lands to Arabs, who, rather than move to the Kurdish area, had leased it to other Kurds. During the uprising, the original Kurdish owners had returned. While bureaucrats became bogged down in intricacies, Cuny, noted for thinking quickly and clearly on his feet, had devised a plan for sharing the harvest that made everyone happy. The Kurds' ability to make it through the fall depended upon the harvest, and the purpose of the fly-over tomorrow was to monitor it. Relief advisors had decided that the number of harvesters in the field the next day was a good barometer for the harvest's success. The military had determined that if there were fifty-two in the field, the Kurds would be in good shape. Cuny and Garner would count the harvesters.

When I awoke early the next morning, Hotel Dahuk was almost dismantled. A quick shower and an MRE (meal ready to eat), and it was time to board the helicopter. I sat by the window so that I could photograph. The helicopter offered a new and exciting perspective of the high mountains and narrow valleys of Kurdistan. We paid a visit to Saddam's palace and overflew the fields. While Garner and Cuny counted the harvesters at work, they commented on the sheer beauty of Kurdistan, what a great place it would be to hike and canoe, how sweet the water was, how cool on a hot day, and, of course, how nice the people were. "I hate to leave them," Cuny said.

"Is it because you're afraid of what's going to happen to them when we're gone?" asked General Garner.

"Yeah." Cuny looked glum.

Many of the allies in Kurdistan shared that fear, and they weren't the first to suffer such worries. The final chapter of *Road Through Kurdistan*, written in 1937 by road builder Archibald Hamilton, had expressed the same well-founded fears when the British left.

Cuny described bringing the Kurds out of the mountains and reestablishing them in northern Iraq as the most successful refugee operation he had worked in. He credited the Kurds themselves for much of the success. "We didn't want to create a dependence we would have to dissolve on leaving, so we tried to serve as consultants to them in making their own system work," he said.

After the uprising, there was no electricity, no water, no medicine. The Kurds had worked industriously from sunup to sunset to open irrigation ditches, terrace gardens, plant tomatoes and eggplant. The allies' first mission had been security; the second, refugee relief—to get food in, restore electricity and water, get the hygienic system up and running, and create employment. Twenty-five Marines had been worked down to one Marine and twenty-four locals paid eight dollars a day. Shops that had been looted and torn down were cleaned up, and tomatoes, honey, and eggplant began to arrive from Iran and other parts of Iraq. The allied forces would now be handing the relief system over to the Kurds, various relief organizations, and the United Nations. They then would leave just enough security to make the U.N. happy.

The harvest proved a success. There were exactly fifty-two harvesters at work in the fields. We shared MREs, then left Hotel Dahuk forever.

"Strap in tight, Mary Ann. Secure your cameras and bags," General Garner instructed me. On his last flight from Hotel Dahuk, Garner flew with the doors open, waving goodbye to the thousands who lined the streets and fields as we overflew the area. Then he told the pilot, "Take us to Amadiya."

While Amadiya was safe and had an idyllic, almost Camelot quality about it, Cizre, just across the Tigris River in Turkey, was more like Dodge City. The Kadooglu Hotel was the coffee shop and gossip stop for Kurdish militants, smugglers, and Turkish police alike, as well as home away from home for journalists and assorted human rights activists. The hotel's balconies overlooked Cizre's main square, a convenience for photographers who from the comfort of their rooms could catch shoot-'em-ups several times a week between the militant Kurdistan Workers' Party (PKK) and Turkish special troops. The square was frequented by photogenic shepherds and their small flocks, along with a pristine white armored vehicle, dubbed "the Turkish wedding tank" by some irreverent Brits. Members of the hotel staff were friendly and helpful, although they were known to cut Turkish journalists' lines just as they were ready to transmit photographs to Paris or London. That was fair, for when skirmishes went badly for the Turks, all of Cizre went dark immediately.

While in Cizre to use the telephone and mail letters, I was enticed by Ragip Duran, a Turkish journalist with whom I had traveled through Kurdish Turkey, to join him at a wedding that evening. Ragip had a soft spot for Cizre and wanted to arrange for it to become a sister city of a Texas border town, having been convinced by movies that Cizre belonged to that genre. The idea seemed right, and I caught myself humming a Texas-Mexican border *corrido* about "*rinches y contrabandistas*," governmental agents and smugglers, folks who complicate the lives of the almost-law-abiding citizens of small border towns such as Cizre, be they in Turkey or in Texas.

After the wedding, we shared refreshments at an open-air tea house on the banks of the Tigris with a local journalist. As we talked, light began to spew and foam near the wedding reception. Just as I pointed out the fireworks, a similar light show began on the other side of the Tigris. "That is not a fireworks display; it is a fire-fight between the PKK and the Turks," said Ragip, calmly sipping his tea as the lights clashed over our heads.

"Then if you will excuse me, I am going to hit the ground," I pronounced politely, explaining that the custom in Texas border towns is to get our heads down when the gunfire starts. Maybe one hundred fifty men at the tea house followed my lead. The sky lit up in a brilliant, wondrous fire display for about twenty minutes. When it was over, we walked to our car, turned on the interior lights, and drove slowly back to the hotel.

"We want both sides to be able to see that we are journalists and not a party to the shooting," Ragip explained. The hotel was chaotic. Electricity was out, phone lines were down, and journalists were frantic. Before anyone could get a line out of Cizre, the BBC was running its report from Ragip's cellular phone. We learned that there had been simultaneous PKK attacks in Sirnak and Silopi, so we headed out for those towns the next morning.

Turkish troops had closed the road to Sirnak, but we found ample evidence of the attack in Silopi, a dusty one-street town near the Iraqi border. A government building was destroyed, and fierce war whoops of women among the attacking PKK rang out from a colleague's dim videotape. Silopi had been a hot spot since the March 1990 uprising in the area. The establishment of the American tent city on the outskirts of the feisty little town had not calmed fighting between the Kurdish militant PKK and Turkish special forces.

Guards at the entrance to the American tent encampment just outside Silopi denied that they had seen anything, but some guys from Tennessee, who were sipping orange drinks at a tarpaulin-covered snack shop next to the base, said that they had been ordered to their tents when the shoot-out started. It had lasted about forty-five minutes. "We only saw fire once during our three months in Iraq. Here in Silopi the skies light up three times a week," one of them told us. "And we're sure going to watch what we pray for. During the Gulf War in Saudi and later in northern Iraq, we prayed to go home or see action. Now we sure wish these fire-fights between the Turks and the PKK—the guys call them the Silopi Offensive—would stop."

"Madame," Aisha said as she arrived breathless in my room one morning, "Father says that you and he are being invited to a very important party tomorrow. General Garner will be sending a helicopter for you."

The distaff half of our household spent the rest of the day readying me for the big event. Our host would be Omar Serchi, the chief of the Serchi tribe, who, the ladies said, was *very* rich. We would be going to Kalakin, Serchi's home high in the mountains, next to Spilik Pass, above Guli Ali Bek, overlooking the Hamilton Road. I knew Omar from his visits with Mr. Ali at the hotel. Once he had brought me a beautiful sheer green Kurdish dress and a light-blue coat covered with sequins, a present in gratitude for all that the Americans had done for the Kurds.

I would be leaving the Badinan, where the Kurmanji dialect of Kurdish was used, and traveling to the area where Sorani was spoken. Leila wanted to prepare me properly for the transition.

"*Gelek sipas nah:* zor *sipas,* zor zor *sipas,*" she laughed. She found saying *zor* or *zor zor sipas* instead of *gelek sipas* for "thank you very much" very funny. "*Zor*" seemed a weird sound to her. Even stranger to Leila was the role of women in the Sorani area, where some of her counterparts mixed freely with men and might be teachers, doctors, or lawyers. A few were even peshmerga, an idea Leila found totally ludicrous.

"You, me, peshmerga," she tried her English, while unloading a phantom Kalashnikov into the enemy, "*Ak-ak-ak-ak-ak-ak-ak*!" Leila laughed, hugged me, then took my hand and had the young peshmerga who attended her bring us tea.

The next morning a helicopter arrived to take Mr. Ali and me to the party. After a thirty-minute ride, we landed near Kalakin at a spot full of helicopters bringing guests. General Garner had ferried over a host of disaster workers who were being honored by Omar for the fine work they had done for the Kurds. Dubbed "J.R." by the Americans because of his opulent lifestyle, Omar laid out a most impressive spread of lamb, fish, saffron-flavored rice, and fruits and vegetables of every variety, delicacies very much appreciated under the circumstances. Omar had a self-sufficient household, organized like that of a medieval castle, perched high on a hill above Kalakin village, and had no trouble producing such luxuries. Every room in Omar's luxurious house was draped with layer upon layer of plush oriental carpets. The party took place outside in a large covered pavilion where we sat on bright orange and yellow tribal rugs placed atop cement benches.

Omar was enchanted with the young female aid workers. He announced that he should very much like to take the entire female aid community as his fourth wife. We could hardly help but applaud that suggestion. We all knew that the Americans would be leaving soon and that this probably was our last party together. "We sent my helicopter from village to village to take the vote, and you were unanimously elected Ms. Kurdistan," General Garner teased me. In a few short months Garner had mastered teatime diplomacy and set the friendly tone that would characterize Kurdish-American relations throughout the relief effort.

It was time for the Americans and allies to leave Zakho. True, they were only going to Silopi, just across the Turkish border, "just a phone-call away," according to General Shalikashvili. Nevertheless, the air was tense as the last allied checkpoint closed and equipment and truckloads of men headed across the bridge at Habur. Last across were the officers on foot, led by General Garner. Zakho was quiet for a day, then, feeling the freedom of an adolescent whose parents have just left town, became a lively Middle Eastern border town once more.

# 3
# THE VIOLATED VILLAGES
July 1991


Peshmerga after peshmerga were arriving at the once fine resort hotel that served as headquarters for the Patriotic Union of Kurdistan (PUK) in Shaqlawa. Hundreds of Land Cruisers lined up to discharge their passengers, each of whom wore the baggy trousers of the peshmerga and carried a Kalashnikov. They ascended the steps, walked through the lobby, and down onto the vast lawn that spread between the hotel and the city. Behind this mass of black-and-white-turbaned humanity rose a line of noble Kurdish mountains. I descended the steps and walked around behind the men, who numbered about ten thousand. From the back of the crowd, I could barely see Jalal Talabani, the leader of the PUK, who was speaking from the terrace.

"Hi," a shy feminine voice said. Looking around, I spied an attractive slim woman, her black hair just beginning to gray, clad in a tan peshmerga outfit, balancing a video camera on a rock. She was Hero Talabani, wife of the speaker. "My tripod is broken, and I forgot my telephoto lens," she complained, fidgeting with her camera.

Hero sat at ease, intent on her videotaping, the lone Kurdish woman among the horde of men. When the meeting was over, we picked up our respective camera gear, braved two long flights of stairs, and shared tea and conversation on the veranda.

"My Kurdish friends wear traditional dresses and don't sit with men in public. You dress like the peshmerga and are often at Jalal's side," I said.

Hero smiled and looked me in the eyes "Women everywhere often are at fault for their own situations. I tell young women, 'Don't be your grandmother. Be your own woman.' To matrons, I say, 'Educate your daughters. Don't make them servants of your sons.' Many Kurdish women are engineers, doctors, attorneys. Men honor those choices, but women must recognize their own worth first."

"How do you work with the peshmerga?" I boldly inquired.

"The peshmerga respect you when you do as they do, live as they live. At first it was hard. During my first march I prayed 'Dear God, just let me keep going.' But when you give your all, when you live like the peshmerga, they accept you as one of them."

"Do you consider yourself a peshmerga?"

"Definitely. I came here with Jalal in 1980. When I saw the situation, I knew I must stay. My youngest boy was a baby; my elder, seven. I left them with my parents in London to fight for my people."

"Do you carry a Kalashnikov?"

"No," she laughed. "But not because I am a woman," she insisted. "I hurt my collarbone in an automobile accident. An attack rifle would be too heavy for me. As a fighter, I would be a nuisance."

"So you videotape?"

"Yes. I have tapes of many battles, many camps and villages."

"I've wanted to go to one of the peshmerga camps and live there for a while, to see how they operate," I confessed.

"Why don't you go with my father and me? He is visiting me from London and wants to see his sisters who live in Suleymaniye. We leave tomorrow for our new camp in Qala Chwalan. You are welcome to join us. It's the worst part of Iraq. Everything has been demolished. The bases we won from Saddam are bad, but we had to let people live in them."

Hero's father is Ibrahim Ahmad, a legendary writer noted for having introduced liberal political thought to Kurdistan. I quickly accepted her invitation and was at the Talabani home early the next morning. Four Land Cruisers stood in a line in front of the house. A friendly peshmerga loaded me into the front of the second. Hero's father climbed into the back. His step was lively, even with his cane, and years had not dimmed a twinkle in his eyes. He wore a peshmerga suit but didn't cover his balding head with a turban. His smile was straightforward, his manner relaxed. Hero boarded last, somewhat flustered from the trip preparations, but very much in command.

"I always think I will forget something," she said.

We were off, I in the front seat with the driver and my cameras, father and daughter in back with water, lemonade, and cookies for the journey. A Land Cruiser of armed peshmerga went in front and two followed. The human cargo was precious and its safety not to be left to chance.

Fifteen minutes out of Shaqlawa, the road wound through a lush green meadow filled with babbling brooks and shaded by poplars. What appeared to have been a town was now piles of gray rubble. Children played on the grass, and young men cooled Pepsis in the stream. A few stands peddled soft drinks to travelers. "Heran was a town of about five hundred houses. Kurdish songs celebrate the pomegranates of Heran and nearby Nazanin. Saddam couldn't destroy them with bulldozers as he had others, so he blew them up with TNT in 1987," Hero said sadly.

A few minutes farther down the road, we passed the remains of Nazanin, then the rubble that once was Nezihan. "Saddam destroyed twenty-eight villages in this valley alone," Hero remarked. "Kurds are a village people. The villages were the backbone of our society. By destroying them, Saddam hoped to obliterate our way of life. He decided to destroy all Kurdish villages, to let only our cities remain. Step by step, he carried out his plan. Step by step, he destroyed our villages and sent the Kurds to concentration camps."

We continued through fields of golden wheat punctuated by piles of rubble. "This is Sheikh Wasan," she pointed to ruins, "the first village in which chemical weapons were used. People ran to their shelters, the worst place they could go. Most people and all the animals died. Some people went to Erbil for treatment and were killed to hush up the story. This happened almost two years before the massive chemical slaughter of Kurds at Halabja. We told every-one that we could. We tried desperately to get help, to spare more of our people this ghastly death. But no one believed us."

Kurdistan had suffered tens of thousands of homes destroyed, hundreds of thousands of people displaced, a way of life snuffed out with few to witness the pain of its passing.

"Iraqi officials wanted to Arabize these villages," said Hero, pointing to heaps of rocks we were passing. "So they imported Iraqi Arabs and Egyptians, who soon became unhappy and left for cities."

Our road dead-ended into a highway. "This is the last pesh-merga checkpoint. Those are Saddam's men over there," Hero said, pointing to tents on a hill about half a mile away.

After experiencing so much destruction, the dust and bustle of Ranya was a welcome affirmation of humanity. We stopped to buy food, inspect our cars, and enjoy soft drinks. Over a mountain, not far from Ranya, an azure lake appeared. It was framed by yellow mountains just beyond fields of leafy greens that alternated with fields of sun-flowers, creating a beautiful patchwork of aqua and green and gold.

"I learned to hate those flowers during the war." Hero laughed. "At night we would march through the sunflowers. They are strong and hard, and I am short. They hit me right in the face. The lake is man-made. It backs up against Dukan Dam to provide water for southern Iraq. It doesn't help the Kurds a bit. Beneath it is some of our most fertile land and, of course, more villages."

We drove downhill to the lake. The ferry was stuck on the other side, unable to discharge a tractor/trailer. "It looks as if this will take awhile. We'd best eat," Hero said. We found shelter from the sun in a small building with one wall missing. Two peshmerga chopped tomatoes and cucumbers, another set plates on a colorful oilcloth. While Hero's father caught the news on his radio, she unwrapped some cooked kebab meat. "It's not like the feasts you enjoyed at your friend J.R.'s house, Mariana," laughed Hero, "but now you will learn how we poor peshmerga live."

We downed Pepsis with our meal, had tea, then reboarded the Land Cruiser. As we crossed Dukan Lake, Ibrahim Ahmad smiled at me mischievously. "When you are on a strange journey in a strange land among strange men, you must try everything once," he insisted. With that he dramatically produced a bright pink Kurdish ice refreshment from behind his back. The peshmerga laughed.

The road on the other side of the lake had been bombed into misshapen bits. The mountains grew higher and more yellow. Rock piles, one after another, marked the sites of villages that had once thrived in this area. We stopped at the foot of a large mountain in Maluma, a village where pieces of several buildings had survived.

"You see that cave up there." Hero's father pointed midway up the mountain. "It was my home, my refuge from the Iraqi regime, for two years in the 1960's." Months after he was reported dead, Ahmad had been discovered by a surprised British journalist who announced that Ahmad was safe in a cave in Kurdistan, writing his memoirs and reading the works of Dostoevski.

A few villagers wandered by. "They live in the hospital over there," Ahmad pointed to a badly damaged building, "and fifteen families are living in the remains of the schoolhouse."

A woman invited us for tea. Her home, nestled among some trees, consisted of part of a wall, several carpets, blankets, and some kitchen utensils. A tree served as the roof. "This is all that is left of my house," she told us. "The tree protects us from the sun. Before winter, we must build something more."

Twenty minutes down the road another village appeared. People were living in tents and huts fashioned of tree limbs. "This is Balik," said Ahmad, "an old town on a trade route established when this area was part of the Ottoman Empire. Saddam destroyed Balik and sent villagers to concentration villages or to southern Iraq. Those who could fled to the mountains and Iran. But with the March uprising families returned to rebuild. Kurdistan and its villages will not be destroyed; the Kurds cannot be stopped easily."

Would the rebuilt villages band into an independent nation?

Ibrahim Ahmad was pensive. "Not even in a dream do I think of a separate, united Kurdistan. The people of the Middle East have more in common with each other that those of Britain, Germany, and

Italy. The distinction between Arabs and Kurds came with Western nationalism. Ethnic minorities—Kurds, Christians, and Jews—had more freedom in the days of the Ottoman Empire than they do now. We need more unity in this part of the world, not more division.

"Chauvinistic ideas will never succeed. The realistic way to deal with people is as brothers without giving importance to their religion or language. Otherwise, the world will become a jungle. Democracy is the answer for this region."

Ahmad smiled frequently as he chatted affectionately with the villagers, who were genuinely happy to see him. "I was their lawyer and got their land back from the tribal chiefs. The Iraqi government sentenced me to jail for two years for defending these people and forbade me to ever come back here. Now I am back," Ibrahim Ahmad sighed with a smile. "And so are my beautiful people."

"How long will you stay in Kurdistan?" I inquired.

"Only a month this visit," he answered. "If Hero's mother gives me permission, I shall return. But she must agree. In our family we believe in democracy, not as an idea but as a tradition."

We bumped past more destroyed villages, past two peshmerga camps, and arrived at Qala Chwalan, once the capital of the emirate of Baban, now reduced to a few battered buildings. We turned down a dirt road between the buildings, and a peshmerga opened a barrier for us. To our right stood a long cinder block dormitory. Directly ahead was headquarters, a one-story building faced with cut stone.

"The camp was miserable when we first arrived," Hero said. "What the shelling didn't destroy, the people here did. They tore out ceilings and walls. Iraqi soldiers had forced them out of their houses without allowing them to take anything with them. They were angry and irrational when they attacked the fort."

Inside, headquarters was stark but clean. The floors were worn terrazzo, the walls plaster. The ceiling, indeed, had been torn out, leaving pieces of steel and the building materials exposed. Furniture was sparse and battered.

"Take your rest," invited Hero, showing me to a room void of furniture except for a carpet and blankets and pillows in a corner. "I'm afraid this is all that we poor peshmerga can offer."

The heat made resting difficult. Women in flowing Kurdish dresses entered the room next to mine. Perhaps they were Ibrahim Ahmad's sister and her family from Suleymaniye, I thought. Unable to fight the heat, I went outside on the back steps to write. Shortly, a peshmerga came and put down a rug, pillows, and one chair. The other guests joined me on the porch.

A woman in her early eighties with striking white hair, clad in an elegant black-and-white traditional dress, sat stiffly on the chair, a black-velvet pillbox studded with rhinestones tied beneath her chin. Two turquoise rings adorned her slender fingers; a tasteful, but substantial gold chain fell to her waist. Her daughter wore a long, diaphanous dress in a tangerine print, a short black sequined jacket typical of the region, and a white scarf draped smartly about her shoulders. Her head was bare. Hero sat on the carpet in peshmerga garb, legs crossed and knees under her chin, pursuing an animated political discussion with the women. Ibrahim Ahmad half reclined on a cushion, systematically reading a formidable pile of newspapers, listening to the BBC on his ever-present shortwave radio, and absent-mindedly assassinating flies with a bright orange fly swatter.

Three teenage girls sat to one side. The eldest, who was about eighteen years old wore a white blouse and straight black skirt, a conservative but stylish outfit. Her hair was pulled back with a black silk bow, revealing pretty gold bow-shaped earrings. She radiated an intelligence and determination worthy of her Aunt Hero. The two younger girls, dressed in denim skirts and T-shirts, would have been at home in an American shopping mall.

"Don't be your grandmother," Hero had said in Shaqlawa. Each woman here was certainly, confidently her own woman.

After taking tea, I ventured out for a walk. Close behind me came the young women.

"Why are you here? Do you like Kurdistan? Have you girls our age at home?"

"And you ladies, are you studying? What do you want to be?"

"An engineer." "A teacher." "A lawyer."

These girls, who obviously loved and respected their elders, were definitely not their grandmothers. Nor were they their mothers nor their Aunt Hero. Their mother later told me that they wanted to be peshmerga, but they insisted that they didn't. Although they loved Kurdistan, they were not ready to take up arms and die for it.

"What sort of man would you like to marry?" I inquired.

"I haven't thought about that," the eldest said thoughtfully. "I've been too busy studying to think of marriage."

After breakfast the next morning, Hero and I sat on the floor and watched her videotapes. "My hand was shaking, even my mind was shaking. I had lived in that village. I knew the people," said Hero as we watched her video of the bombing of a village. "Each time I film an attack, something happens to my mind. It makes me crazy," she said as the bombing became more intense. "I hurt for my people."

The film jumped as bombs exploded in brilliant purple and yellows. "This happened in the editing," said Hero. "These mistakes are not on the original."

Even colors seemed violated by the bombs. "Don't change it, Hero. It's a new high in cinematic expressionism."

"Here is a village before the bombardment, then during the bombing, and again twenty minutes later. It burned all night long. That's why you can see the trees in the dark." Her tone was somber. "Believe me. I will take pictures while they are rebuilding it."

A fern growing out of a bomb stood in front of a school. "These are Russian bombs. I took pictures of their serial numbers. The village made a planter out of this bomb piece. The writing says in Kurdish, 'A present to our children of Kurdistan from Saddam Hussein and his Ba'ath Party.' "

A very different image appeared of contented villagers cutting wheat with hand scythes and singing. They swayed to and fro in graceful, rhythmic unison. "This is the traditional way we harvest in Kurdish villages. This is our life when we are left in peace." A butterfly flitted across the scene, its flight caught by Hero's astute camera. The contrasts of Hero's videotapes were those of Kurdistan itself, the song of plenty and the lament of loss, butterflies and bombs flying past the majestic yellow mountains, adorning and demolishing the Kurdish villages.

"It was hard to take pictures of the shelling. It went on daily," Hero commented as we saw another village being destroyed with bombs. "There were no peshmerga in that village, only civilians. This was our life in 1984 and 1985." A boy about four years old smiled at us from the video screen. "I asked him, 'Were you afraid?' He said, 'No. But my little sister cried.' These villagers want to pick their tomatoes, but there are cluster bombs in their garden." A bird sang on the video, but then the bombs began again.

"The Iraqis would bombard villages daily to make people leave, to force them into the mountains. But the people would build houses and tents of plastic. When the Iraqis stopped letting food in, the peshmerga would cut back-roads and smuggle it to them. The ruling Ba'ath Party didn't want the outside world to know that they were bombing their own people. The man you see there told me, 'When I took my grandson to the hospital after an air raid, they told me I must say that we were bombed by Iranians or they wouldn't treat the boy. My grandson died anyway, so my lie didn't help him.' "

Children pulled toy cars made of discarded wire and spools across the screen, then the tape cut to a woman making bread. A blind man spoke to the camera, "No one could bring me out of the village or care for me, so I moved to this cave. Somebody told me that his father died a few days ago and that he would bring me his coat. But he didn't."

"The man died soon after this interview," Hero said.

"These children have chemical wounds." Hero pointed to the closeups of children with blistered and burnt skin. "And this video was taken before the well-known tragedy at Halabja. We showed these to our friends, to politicians, to the press to try to get help, to avoid this pain and death. But no one would believe us. No one would help. Look how terrible these wounds are," she said sadly.

Hero provided me with a peshmerga outfit to blend in better with others working close to the cease-fire line between the Kurds and Saddam's troops and sent me with two trusted peshmerga, Kawa and Raoof, to view the remains of Sayid Sadik and Halabja, two towns destroyed by Saddam's troops. Even in extreme distress, Sayid Sadik was lively and colorful. People had returned, burrowed under roofs, added a few stones to existing walls, or simply constructed small huts of tree limbs and leaves atop the rubble. Over fifty thousand refugees fleeing the fighting in Suleymaniye had poured into Sayid Sadik this week. They joined the hundred thousand plus who had returned here after the March rebellion.

Halabja was a wretched mass of twisted, tormented houses and buildings, a monument to the March 1988 attack, when more than five thousand people had been exterminated by chemicals. The terror of the dead and dying that terrible day was reflected in the eyes of the people who remained. A young boy mounted a large bombshell like a toy horse, trying to entice me to take his photograph. "Don't you want to see the mounds where the people are buried?" Kawa asked.

"I just want out of here," I replied.

"Halabshima," a sign read on the main street, equating the nearly total destruction of Halabja to that of Hiroshima. I was told that the Japanese government has recognized Halabja as such and planned to help restore it. But I could not bear to stay and learn more. I could take the destroyed villages; I could take the videos of bombings and chemical wounds; I could take explicit photographs of the tragedy at Halabja, but I could not take the terror in the eyes of the survivors.

I was quiet as we returned to Qala Chwalan. When we arrived Hero asked "How was your day? Did you see enough?"

"I saw too much," I answered honestly.

# 4
# PENJWIN
July 1991

We bumped over bombed-out roads for four hours, then turned onto Penjwin's main street—a dirt road lined with shabby booths that had been quickly set up to sell wares—thus adding traffic congestion to our woes. Trucks were laden with produce, household goods, and even people. Families fleeing the shelling in Erbil and Suleymaniye were arriving by the thousands. Beyond the market, Penjwin, once a thriving town of one hundred and fifty thousand, was nothing but piles of rubble, millions and millions of small stones with a wall here, a roof there, and tents and huts made of leaves and boughs perched atop the ruins.

"Penjwin is like Jerusalem in A.D. 75," a relief worker later told me. "Not one stone left standing upon another. The destruction is epic, biblical in proportion. There is something of the demonic in it. How could such a thing have happened and we not know?"

Penjwin had been bombed and then dynamited by Iraqi troops in September 1963 and again in 1965. In December 1983, when Saddam reduced Penjwin to rubble, some Kurds had been deported to southern Iraq, some taken to government concentration villages. Most fled to the mountains, to Iran, to safety. To discourage their return, the Iraqi government had mined the water pipes under Penjwin, the surrounding fields, and even the springs, acts clearly aimed at the civilian population.

Despite the massive destruction and danger, Kurds had begun to return to their homes in Penjwin. The pitched tents atop some flattened roofs and the hovels burrowed under others attested to their return, as did the multiplicity of leaf-and-bough huts.

We drove through Penjwin and stopped just where the town seemed to end. Samir, a young peshmerga who had escorted me from Qala Chwalan, took my bags and encouraged me down a bluff. We had arrived at Charba, the camp of the famous commander Bekir Haji Safir. Bekir, a handsome man of about fifty wearing a gray peshmerga suit, welcomed us. "Please, come in; take your rest. We will have lunch shortly," he said, ushering us into a thirty-by-forty-foot leaf-

and-bough reception house, the dirt floor covered with bedspreads and worn flat-weave carpets. Kafiya, a striking woman in a flowing traditional Kurdish dress, took her place at her husband's side. Three peshmerga unrolled two brightly patterned oilcloths on the ground and set out a generous meal of rice, wild greens, okra and tomatoes, local herbs, and green onions. Bekir's family and guests, which included women and children who had come for help, sat at one long rectangular cloth. We numbered eighteen. Nineteen peshmerga sat at a second. Over lunch Bekir explained why the Kurds could persist when their homes and villages had been reduced to rubble and their society nearly destroyed.

"Love has enabled us to survive and return here together; caring for one another allows us to continue even though we have no houses and very little food. There are no words to describe my love for my wife Kafiya; she has been at my side for twenty-six years, often fighting in the mountains."

"Men and women fight side by side," Kafiya told me. "We fight so that our children will live safely in a free Kurdistan. All of us are peshmerga, all of us face death for Kurdistan, even the children, who often miss years of school. But not all of the peshmerga fight with guns."

"I fight with my pen," Samir said. "I fight with information, guiding journalists through Kurdistan and translating."

Deil, a ten-year-old refugee from Suleymaniye, wanted to contribute by becoming a teacher of Kurdish. Kafiya's eleven-year-old daughter, Hazia, who was born while her mother was in prison, said she would serve in a more direct manner. "I want to be a pesh-merga like my mom."

"I want to be a pilot and bomb Saddam's palace," Hazia's eight-year-old brother, Hajan, vigorously interjected.

"Last week the government attacked Suleymaniye with tanks," a woman refugee said. "I'm afraid of the tanks. The army of Baghdad has surrounded Suleymaniye. We pray for God and you, the Americans, to help us. People are afraid of a chemical attack. But life here in Charba and Penjwin is better, safer than in the cities. There is food, a hospital. There are no Iraqi tanks attacking."

"It's all very well here right now," said Bekir. "But will a tent-hospital or our leaf-and-bough huts be so comfortable when the snow is a more than a meter deep?"

I stayed at Bekir's camp for ten days, living in my own leaf-and-bough hut, furnished with piles of blankets and pillows which served both for sitting and for sleeping. Life in a leaf-and-bough hut set

43

amid massive devastation was amazingly pleasant. As Bekir had told me, love and consideration were important weapons in the Kurds' struggle to survive. No one had become short-tempered or mean under these difficult circumstances; hardship had not dampened the generosity and politeness of these mountain people.

Adherence to tradition was important to the Kurds at Charba and Penjwin. Kurds are one of the few groups in the Middle East to maintain their traditional costumes. Even under the most difficult of circumstances, the peshmerga in their baggy pants and colorful cummerbunds managed to look brave. The flowing gowns that the women wore reminded the world that they were elegant, even when under fire or in pain.

During the day Bekir, as political head of Penjwin, spoke with officials and visitors in the large leaf-and-bough reception house. He tried to help them with their problems, heard their complaints, and held a kind of court in which he settled disputes. Bekir knew everyone in the Penjwin area and arranged for me to visit with the many international relief workers charged with rehabilitating Penjwin. One of the most interesting workers I met was Magnus Hullgrimsson of Iceland, a consulting hydrologic engineer with the International Committee of the Red Cross.

Magnus was lanky and wiry, on the young side of middle-aged; he sported glasses and a short, well-trimmed gray beard. He wore a white cotton shirt, hiking shoes, and what looked like a print tablecloth tied around his waist. Magnus was strong, straightforward, and he totally lacked pretension. A smile in his eyes betrayed a great enthusiasm for life and his work, which in this case was to provide water for the area.

"One of the strategies of the destruction was to deny people access to water," he told me. "Water tanks were bombed. Mines were placed around the best springs so that people would be maimed or killed when they came for water. The destruction here was carefully planned and carried out to an extent that is amazing. Such complete demolition is difficult to achieve."

Five Icelanders formed the Red Cross sanitation engineering team in Penjwin. They were in charge of providing drinking water and of cleaning, repairing, and revitalizing the water system. The team provided about half of the water from the badly damaged old system and had harnessed sixty-five springs, which they pumped to distribution sites. These included twelve cylindrical OXFAM tanks (so called because they were developed by the Oxford Famine Relief Organization), fourteen bladders, which looked like giant waterbed mattresses, and one broken-down water tanker. From a tank or bladder the water would flow directly to a spot for washing, be piped to a distribution rack with taps, or act as a filling station for the twenty-two tankers that served areas farther from water sources.

Magnus invited me to join him one afternoon in checking water distribution sites and inspecting springs that might become more sources of water for Penjwin. Our first stop was a heavily populated tent village on the side of a mountain. Here water was piped to a distribution rack, which looks something like a metal sawhorse with six taps. Women lined up to draw water broke into enthusiastic applause as we arrived; they gathered around Magnus to chat. "It's difficult to realize the importance of water to these people, the pain inflicted on them when they are deprived of it," Magnus explained. "This tent town grew up here because of our water collection site. The people camped here just to be close to water."

At our next stop large hoses brought water from a spring on the mountain to a place where women were washing clothes and dishes. The women stopped their chores and joined their children in giving Magnus another hearty round of applause. "The Kurds are a grateful people. They know who brought them water," he said. "One woman told me, 'Water is life. You have brought us life.'"

Aso Omar Muhadin, whom Magnus introduced as his plumber, translator, foreman, Kurdish activist, and right hand, joined us to inspect the springs. As we started up the mountain behind Aso, Magnus apologized, "There are roads to the springs, but I fear they are more for cows than for people." I realized immediately that my rearing in less than mountainous Texas had not adequately prepared me for the fast walk straight upwards. We had not gone far before Aso casually reached out with the staff he was using to climb and picked up a mine in our path. We went but a bit farther before Aso picked up another mine. Not much farther he found another in our path . . . and another and another. Magnus and Aso were walking very quickly, but I was right behind them, putting my feet exactly where theirs had trod. It seemed to me that we were running up the mountain. We stopped for a minute while Magnus and Aso had an intense discussion.

"He said that he was sorry that all of the mines were not cleared but that three people were killed up here yesterday."

"That doesn't make me cheerful," I answered.

"Nor I," said Magnus. "But we're almost there."

The spring, when we arrived, proved pleasant and cool, but Magnus decided not to use it. "They need to get the mines cleaned out of this area before we attempt to harness this spring."

I wholeheartedly agreed.

When we descended, we boarded Magnus' Land Cruiser and went to inspect two more springs, which proved to be more promising. The water was sweet, cool, and welcome after the climbs—and we saw no more mines.

One evening Bekir and his family arranged a surprise for me. We loaded into two battered Land Cruisers and chugged into the purple twilight. The women were decked out in their finest attire, sparkling with sequins and shiny metallic fabrics. Just as dusk faded into darkness a wondrous range of mountains appeared to our right. "Those mountains are in Iran," Bekir informed me. "The border is marked by the trees over there. Tomorrow morning we can walk to Iran if you like."

A few minutes later the Land Cruiser pulled up to a rock house. A similar house sat on either side of it and in front of it. There were no lights and no furniture other than the inevitable rugs, and part of the ceiling was sagging more than a bit. We were greeted with hugs, kisses, introductions, and plenty of love. This was the house of Bekir's son.

Once inside Kafiya smiled and handed me a package. "*Zor sipas*, thank you very much," I said as I unwrapped it. To my delight, my package contained a lovely blue and white sheer gown, silver lamé bloomers, a short black sequined bolero-type jacket, and a flowing white cotton scarf. "*Zor zor joan e*, it's very beautiful. Thank you very much. *Zor sipas*." The women amused themselves helping me dress. We might be in the high mountains of the Iraqi-Iranian border, in a land where the ladies were called upon to fight next to their men as often as not, but dressed in gowns whose sleeves swept the floor, we were not far from Camelot. Bekir's consort might tote a Kalashnikov when the situation demanded, but she was equally adept at knowing how to reign.

We sat tailor-style on pillows on the floor during supper, sometimes leaning on pillows placed against the wall. The laughter and love that filled the room could have belonged to a large, happy family anywhere in the world; the sagging ceiling, the exuberant clothing, and the pile of Kalashnikovs in the corner reminded me that we were in rebel-held Kurdistan, right in the mountains that divided Iran and Iraq.

As we relaxed over tea, Bekir's young son Hajan began to make gestures like a small goat, no doubt in reference to an animal that was penned in the yard. "And how would you like a small goat?" Bekir asked.

"Barbecued," I ventured. "Transformed into a tasty Texas *cabrito*."

Everyone laughed.

After a breakfast of tea, yogurt, and fresh Kurdish bread the next morning, we drove to Banau Suta, a meadow on the Iraqi-Iranian border for a festive *seran*, a Kurdish picnic. The women got out of the cars, all aglow in colored gossamer, sequined gowns and pantaloons, and traipsed across a meadow, carrying baskets, blankets, and all of the accessories for an extraordinary picnic. Hajan and his cousin followed, pulling the recalcitrant goat behind them. We looked like a cross between a medieval procession and a circus act gone astray.

We reached the shade of several rows of tall pine trees, through which a small stream ran. The women spread blankets under the trees then proceeded to unpack plates, glasses, silverware, and cooking utensils, while the men built a fire and helped Hajan slaughter the goat. Soon the women had goat sizzling in pots of oil. We quickly had our first tender taste arranged in small chunks on shish kebab sticks. This was not a *cabrito* I was likely to forget. With so few animals in Kurdistan now, my hosts were truly generous to share this special meal with me. The rest of the goat meat was covered with tomatoes, onions, and vegetables and left to simmer in a large black pot. We sat on our blankets and relished the tasty stew, served over the inevitable rice, and, after tea, spread our blankets on a shady spot by the stream and slept.

After our nap, Kafiya served us tea and produced a tape recorder. As Kurdish music played, Kafiya smiled and began to dance, moving her shoulders up and down in the distinctive movements of the Kurdish *hora*. Her daughters joined arms with her, and the women danced energetically up hill and down for about forty-five minutes, then they collapsed in exhaustion and laughter upon the blankets. Kafiya had her daughters make more tea for us. Raising her cup to me, she smiled, "May all of your days be picnics."

As we sat and sipped tea, listening to Kurdish music, Bekir became serious. He had come to this area in 1963 as a peshmerga; twenty-eight years later he was married and had children, but it all seemed the same. Despite all of the men, women, and children who had been killed, despite all of the suffering and hardship that Kurds had endured, despite all of the bravery and love, there was no progress. Once more the Kurds had no home. "We are still peshmerga and refugees," he said pensively, seated beneath the majestic Kurdish mountains, his wife and his Kalashnikov at his side.

# 5
# SULEYMANIYE

August 1991

Hero was less than enthusiastic about my planned trip to Suleymaniye. Kurdish civilians had taken the city from Saddam's men only two weeks before, and their hold was tenuous. The peshmerga now ruled, but some Iraqi soldiers were still in the city and Saddam's troops, armed with heavy artillery, had it surrounded. At any moment the city might be engulfed in more fighting. Nevertheless, Nazanin, a schoolteacher who had been visiting Hero's peshmerga friend Kafiya Suleman, invited me to accompany her home. If I were to miss this opportunity, I might never have another chance to experience an Iraqi Kurdish city.

"If you insist on going, you must be very careful," warned Hero. "Don't tell a single peshmerga your plans. If Saddam's men were to learn that you are going—and they easily could—you would be picked up in a minute. And there are still Iraqi soldiers at the checkpoint. What if they ask for identification?"

"I've been back and forth three times this week and have been waved through," Nazanin assured Hero.

"That's because you are from here. Mariana is a stranger. She must not be recognized as such. We must disguise her," Hero decided.

My peshmerga outfit wouldn't do. My Kurdish dress was judged "too Badinani," and Kafiya's mother-in-law's dress was "not believable" on me. In any case, a woman my age in a Soran city like Suleymaniye would wear traditional Kurdish clothing only on special occasions. Kafiya produced a pleated navy skirt, Nazanin contributed a print blouse, and Kafiya's mother-in-law fetched me a white scarf. A defeated Hero clasped her head and offered shoes and sunglasses.

"No Kurdish woman would wear your white tennis shoes. Are you *sure* you want to do this?"

"Kafiya is going too," I said.

"Good God! Kafiya has a price on her head!" Hero exclaimed in despair. "Saddam can capture a Kurdish woman leader *and* an American at one try, and both are friends of mine!"

The taxi driver and Kafiya's traditionally dressed mother-in-law sat in front. We three Kurdish schoolteachers in our similar skirts and blouses were in the back seat, I in the middle with my camera equipment in an innocent-looking plastic shopping bag. At the top of the mountain overlooking Suleymaniye we reached the checkpoint. An Iraqi soldier and a peshmerga looked into the car, saw a Kurdish matron and three schoolteachers, and waved us through with no questions.

Iraqi soldiers, tents, and artillery stretched as far as the eye could see. We drove through the troops for twenty minutes. Beneath the berets cocked jauntily to one side were so many mothers' sons, who looked like boy scouts on an outing, too inexperienced to understand the personal tragedies that an all-out attack on the Kurds would bring.

We entered Suleymaniye and left Kafiya and her mother-in-law on a dusty street close to the highway, then drove through a well-kept business section and turned into a pleasant neighborhood. All we could see from the car were sidewalks, stucco walls, and tall wooden gates. When we arrived at her house, Nazanin got out of the car and opened the gate. Thick stucco walls flush with the sidewalk opened onto an attractive patio filled with flowers and plants. The one-story white stucco house sat to the back. Plaster walls were painted in tasteful pastels, and the floors were well-kept terrazzo splashed with oriental rugs. Her living room was spacious, furnished with over-stuffed velvet and mahogany sofas and chairs, and a mahogany-and-glass chest full of mementos of Venice, Rome, and Czechoslovakia. Among her international treasures were records from America. "America is our salvation," Nazanin told me. "I use Frank Sinatra records to teach my Kurdish friends about America. They learn American idioms, music, and culture along with the words. I know all of the words to many songs by Frankie, but 'Strangers in the Night' is my favorite.

"Strangers in the night, exchanging glances/ wondering in the night what were the chances/ we'd be sharing love before the night was through . . . ." Nazanin recited dramatically, appearing to be a love-struck lady and a school teacher all at once. "Things turned out all right for strangers in the night," she finished the song.

I had learned Spanish from Mexican love songs and well remembered how much those romantic classics had confused some Americans about life and customs south of the border. What were Kurds learning from Frank Sinatra? Certainly that when inflamed, we commit like no others to the quick fix. Sinatra's words reinforced Kurdish attitudes towards Americans. American soldiers had been prominent in the international effort to bring the Kurds safely out of their mountain camps and resettle them in the Safe-haven; an American colonel coordinated the on-going relief effort; American planes stationed across the border at Incirlik, Turkey, continued to overfly the area and protect the Kurds. Kurds wanted to believe that Americans loved them and could offer permanent answers to much more complex questions. Like adolescents they risked mistaking impassioned glances for longtime commitment.

Nazanin wanted to join the peshmerga in the mountains like her friends Kafiya and Hero, but it was impossible for a single woman to do so. She worked for the Kurdish resistance in the city, teaching adults as well as young people about Kurdistan and the West. She often taught in an indirect manner; she had to be careful what she said.

"The Iraqis allow us a sense of freedom now. When the allies leave Kurdistan, we are all dead, and we know it. Ali Hasan al-Magid, Minister of the Interior, Saddam's cousin, is in Kirkuk. He was the first to use chemical weapons, and he engineered the destruction of Halabja. The school children call him Ali Chemical."

Nazanin planned a tour of the city to visit her friends and colleagues. Hero and Kafiya were special, Nazanin explained; they understood things in a way that other Kurds could not. It was important to her that I see how average citizens lived and perceived their situation. Her nephew would drive us, and his younger brother would go along so that we would appear to be a family outing. We would tour right after lunch, while it was still hot, before the after-noon crowds gathered, to avoid attracting attention.

Suleymaniye was a clean, attractive city with broad avenues and modern buildings. Statues attesting to the glory of Saddam stood in the middle of flower-filled traffic circles. An occasional destroyed building, another riddled with bullets, and armed peshmerga in the street were the only signs of the recent uprising. When we stopped at Nazanin's friends' house for tea, we pulled the car into their patio and closed the gate behind us. These  precautions were taken in consideration of those whom I was visiting. Were Saddam to retake the town, they could be severely punished for having received me.

Nazanin's friends offered us an orange-flavored drink, which was very welcome on this hot day. "Why haven't the Americans helped here?" the husband asked. "I worry about  the people in the villages. I worry about the children here."

"Our commitment was only to get the Kurds out of the mountains on the borders and provide protection for them to return home," I chanted like an American parrot.

"That protection should have extended to Suleymaniye," he insisted. "When Haji Bush asked Iraqis to rise up against Saddam, we obeyed. Haji Bush himself issued the call to arms. I heard him on radio and television several times. Many people have been hurt here. The situation became so bad that the people themselves drove Saddam's troops out of Suleymaniye without waiting for the help of the peshmerga.

"I sometimes doubt the sincerity of the great America to make any real changes in the Middle East. Perhaps you just want a hobbled Saddam, one whom you can control. Or a Saddam clone. A real change, one that would help the people, might not be to America's advantage."

We thanked our hosts, said our goodbyes, then were off. We crossed a main thoroughfare into what was still called the Jewish neighborhood, although most Iraqi Jews had left when Israel was formed. Nazanin thought that they were lucky to get out, given Saddam's treatment of minorities, such as Kurds and Jews. She looked at the dilapidated neighborhood in disgust. "This is not Suleymaniye; this is filth. Look at these people sitting in the dust."

The streets in the old neighborhood were dirt. People sat in front of their houses in the afternoon, probably to escape the heat and the smells of badly ventilated buildings, and did not seem afraid. Some cleaned the street around their houses; some baked bread. These were the people in Suleymaniye with the least to lose; somehow that made them freer and less afraid.


We drove on to the market. "Look at our children selling fruit," complained Nazanin. "There is no work. We are reduced to having our children sell things on the street."

"This doesn't look so bad as the villages," I felt compelled to say. "At least there is fruit to sell."

"Perhaps not. This is how things are all through Kurdistan. But it was not always like this, Mariana. And it gets worse and worse. As a schoolteacher, I cannot help but be sad for these children."

As we turned onto the main street, we saw twenty or so Iraqi soldiers. Farther down the street, six more soldiers were standing on a street corner. We turned right, pulled into a driveway, and stopped in front of a two-story brown brick building. "This is my school," Nazanin announced.

"I don't think we should get out here, Nazanin. The soldiers are too close."

"It's my school, Mariana." Nazanin insisted, "They'll think we are two teachers come to check the school building."

I got out of the car cautiously, my mind fixed on the soldiers around the corner. While Nazanin walked confidently towards the school, I approached slowly, looking over my shoulder frequently to see if we had been noticed or were being followed. My apprehension continued even after we entered the building and shut the door behind us. A long hallway was quiet and smelled of dust and chalk, very like those of July schoolhouses throughout much of the world; classrooms lined up on the left, and light entered from dingy windows on the right. Nazanin marched into the rooms one by one like a general inspecting the damage after a battle. "What animal would smash the children's chalkboards?" she asked accusingly, pointing at the small remains of what had once been a slate board, stubbornly clinging to the wall in the first classroom. "And leave the children with no place to sit and do their work?" she added, as we surveyed smashed parts of what had been student desks. "Why would soldiers destroy the student's musical instruments and school books?" she continued, pointing to the broken and torn remnants of teaching tools stacked high in the corner of one classroom. "In order to totally obliterate Kurdish society, Saddam stooped to shattering the world of children, to stopping their education. We have no money to replace the chalkboards, no means to buy more schoolbooks, no new musical instruments for the children. Only monsters would stoop to ravishing the children's schools," Nazanin concluded.

The vandalized school rooms with their broken desks and equipment were sad, but I found it hard to mourn smashed chalkboards while vivid memories of the dynamited schools in the villages lingered in my head. And I was somewhat more than distracted by thoughts of the soldiers we had seen on the street.

"Nazanin, what if those soldiers saw us come in here and decide to check our identification?"

"I don't care, Mariana. This is my school, and I shall come here when I wish," she insisted, "just as the peshmerga come and go as they wish in the mountains."

But the peshmerga were many, and we were two; the peshmerga had arms, and we had none. I now clearly realized why Hero had been so concerned about my visit to Suleymaniye: Nazanin's laudable heroism could very well get me picked up as a spy. I thought about how unhappy I would be speaking to my children via the evening news as other Western prisoners had had to do. Nevertheless, I acquiesced to Nazanin's request to continue our tour. The resigned, silent anxiety that I experienced as we examined the rest of the battered schoolhouse made me understand that the fears of sudden disappearance and incarceration that Kurdish city folk suffered were equally as difficult as the villagers' preoccupation with chemical weapons and bomb attacks.

After we left the school, we visited another home. "Please don't take pictures of our children," said our hostess, offering me an orange drink. She feared being identified with me. She may also have feared being identified *by* me. "Don't take my picture. Don't use my name. Don't quote me. I didn't say anything," the family whispered as *Sesame Street* in Arabic gave way to televised mosque prayers.

"We must get the word to the West. Mariana must see normal life," objected Nazanin.

But I was seeing normal life. *Sesame Street* and televised mosque prayers, doilies and dollies and whatnots, overstuffed furniture and orange-flavored soft drinks were the accouterments of the bourgeois Hell of which Nazanin spoke. The garden abundant with flowers and the big-screen television did not allay the terrible fears, the terror of being suddenly swept away.

We picked up Kafiya, her mother-in-law, and added two little girls to our car, in order to appear to be a happy family. As we left the highway circling Suleymaniye and crossed into the area dominated by Iraqi soldiers, the little girls began to twitch and squirm. Fear and anxiety invaded their faces. Their nervous expressions revealed what Nazanin's words had not been able to do: One of the Iraqi regime's major objectives was to plant terror in the hearts of children. Ever the schoolteacher, Nazanin started a chanting game, singing and clapping. The girls joined in, nervously at first. As they concentrated on the game, the fear disappeared from their faces. As their eyes focused on the other participants, the nervous twitching stopped. Soon they became lost in the song, although one still watched the soldiers from the corner of her eye. We passed the troops and reached the final checkpoint. The singing schoolteachers and little girls were waved through with a smile from both the peshmerga and the Iraqi soldier.

When I arrived at headquarters in Qala Chwalan, the peshmerga were sitting on the floor watching a videotape of the movie *Johnny Texas*. Cowboys did not charm them like Frank Sinatra had Nazanin. "We don't want to visit you in Texas," they announced. "The guys there pack too many guns." The peshmerga laughed, and I laughed too. But as I thought through my day in the city, I realized that I wasn't frightened of the guys with the guns, the cowboys and the peshmerga. It was the city politicians, the men armed with words, the "strangers in the night" who had me worried.

# 6
# QALA CHWALAN

August 1991

Perched on a flat-weave cloth rug in the entrance hall of the Patriotic Union of Kurdistan headquarters in Qala Chwalan, her legs and feet curled beneath her, Hero spent a bright summer morning receiving visitors, consoling widows, and directing housekeeping. Her small frame clad in the usual baggy khaki trousers, tan cotton shirt, and short tan jacket, she was part pixie, part peshmerga, part Kurdish matriarch. Talabani headquarters had been moved out of the Safe-haven to entice press into the more dangerous and less accessible rebel-held territory of the southeast, and it provided more comforts for the satellite phone, fax machine, and video equipment than for the human inhabitants. The fifteen-by-eighteen-foot entry hall, which served Hero as reception room by day and bedroom by night, was furnished with a rug and cushions on one side and a small iron bed covered with mosquito netting on the other. Bare bulbs hanging overhead provided light when electricity was available. Steel rods jutted through the ceiling.

"It was worse other times," Hero smiled over tea while hemming curtains between visitors. "Once, Jalal and I lived in one room in the mountains; it was bedroom, kitchen, dining, reception, office, and satellite room—everything but bathroom. We had no doors or windows, only plastic stretched across holes. Our small generator had only enough power for the satellite phone, so we ate our dinner by candlelight.

"Once I even made a toilet. I built it of stone and mud, then covered it with plastic. I put plastic on both sides of a cardboard door, so that rain could not ruin it, and then attached a cord on each side to make a handle. I told friends in London that I was a second Robinson Crusoe."

A man in stately robes arrived with an impressive entourage. As Hero received them inside, the peshmerga sawed, hammered, and painted outside. Equipped with a large, loud cement mixer, some of them poured a slab in front of their barracks; others baked bread in a primitive mud oven. Just outside of the camp, new trainees praised peshmerga life in crisp rhythms as they marched.

*We are the peshmerga, brave heroes of Kurdistan.*
*We will never lay down our arms.*
*We fight until victory or death.*

After Hero's visitor left, four peshmerga arrived carrying two banquet-sized wooden tables. Hero had them placed end-to-end in an empty room at the end of the hall and began to cover the tables with a cloth. Hero had designed the conference table, and the peshmerga had constructed it. "You learn to do everything under these conditions. Soon we shall have a proper headquarters." She laughed.

Over tea, we discussed her impressive visitor, who, Hero explained to me, was one of the most powerful men in the area, a religious as well as a political figure. He often visited her and treated her as if she were his own daughter. While some tribal chiefs and religious leaders kept the women of their family in private quarters, or Ottoman-style harems, the Talabanis had a different arrangement, Hero said.

"One of the best thing Jalal has done for Kurdish women is to include me in meetings. In many places, I have been the first woman to sit in the council room with men. Jalal is really very courageous. It isn't so easy to include your wife in political gatherings in Kurdistan. Sometimes when he is going to a tribal assembly he says, 'Hero, come along,' and I say, 'Oh, my God!' but he insists. By including me, Jalal has made it easier for other men to bring their wives."

I retired to the kitchen to help peshmerga chop tomatoes while Hero received three women. After they left Hero was pensive. "That poor woman has lost her brother, her husband, and now her son. So many Kurds have disappeared without a trace. This kind of life is *ver*y hard on women. When a baby is born in jail, a mother will name the child *Diel*, which means prisoner. Children born in the mountains might be named *Awara*, which means refugee. Many children born during chemical bombardments are called *Kimewe*, which means chemical. Children's names often tell the story of a Kurdish mother and her feelings. Many children have been named Danielle Mitterrand, after the French president's wife, out of gratitude for what she has done for the Kurds, and, in appreciation for America's help, I hear that we are beginning to have young Haji Bushes."

I had noticed that the peshmerga usually put the title *kak* in front of names when addressing one another and asked Hero about that practice.

"All of the peshmerga call each other *kaka or kak*, 'brother,' no matter what their rank. There is no wall between leaders and peshmerga; we are very close to one another. Some very popular peshmerga leaders like Mam Rustum are called *mam*, 'uncle,' out of affection and respect. Except my husband, Jalal. He was named for his uncle Jalal and has been called Mam Jalal since he was a baby. And I can tell that the peshmerga like you, Mariana, because they are starting to call you Auntie Mary Ann."

Suddenly the door sprang open, slamming against the wall, and a handsome, rugged peshmerga with curly hair entered the room, talking loudly and making big gestures. Both he and Hero burst out laughing: Mam Rustum had arrived. "This man yelling, 'Where is the old woman?' is Rustum Mohammed Rahim, twenty-two years a peshmerga, one of Kurdistan's finest warriors," Hero said. "Saddam has a very high price on his head, but we are confident that no one will ever collect it. Rustum has so much metal in him that he could never pass through airport security in Europe."

"Here," he pointed to his leg; "here," to his foot; "here and here and here." Rustum looked as if he were playing tic-tac-toe with his body as he showed me his wounds.

"What does Rustum mean in English?" I asked.

"Rambo," he answered with a big smile.

"Actually, it does," giggled Hero. "Rustum is a warrior hero in Persian legends."

"Rustum Rambo Kirkuki."

"He says he is Rustum Rambo from Kirkuk."

"When will he take me to Kirkuk?" I asked, knowing that it was held by government forces. Rustum acted out his machine gunning and my photographing. From his pantomime it was obvious that a trip to Kirkuk would not be a problem.

Hero still wouldn't go to Suleymaniye. While it was only a thirty-minute drive over the mountains, Saddam's men were there, and Hero was someone they would especially like to capture. But one day a young peshmerga from Suleymaniye came to visit; he and Hero argued in the kitchen, and he left smiling. "That peshmerga." Hero shook her head. "He and his girlfriend have wanted to marry for many years, and finally her brothers have consented. They didn't think that a peshmerga would make a good husband; we haven't much money, you know," she laughed. "Long ago I promised that I would be a witness at his wedding, so tomorrow night we will attend a peshmerga wedding in Suleymaniye."

The next afternoon we packed into a Land Cruiser. Another went behind and two in front of us. Hero was dressed in her pesh-merga clothes, her pistol strapped on her belt. Her face was calm, but she smoked a lot as we drove over the mountains, past the checkpoint, through Saddam's men into Suleymaniye. We could hear a loudspeaker blaring wedding music at least a block before we arrived at the house. As soon as we were out of the Land Cruiser, Hero was whisked away to sit with the bride in the garden. Upstairs in the house, women dressed in long gowns glistened with sequins of all colors; the party dresses of Suleymaniye's women were the most spectacular in all Kurdistan. On a balcony a band played electronic instruments; armed peshmerga stood on the wall that fronted onto the street, Kalashnikovs on the ready. Kurdish men in peshmerga garb and women in fanciful gowns danced arm in arm in a circle in the front of the garden; the bride, clad in a red sequined Kurdish bride's dress sat at the back. She excused herself and returned dressed in the white dress of a Western bride. Her sisters and friends began to place gold jewelry on her—a necklace, pins, bracelets; Hero put golden earrings on her ears. A smiling groom slipped a golden bracelet on his bride's arm, a golden ring on her finger, then took her by the hand to join the dancers.

"We want to thank Hero Talabani," a man said over the loudspeaker, and the guests burst into applause. Hero smiled from her seat. "We are so proud to have Hero Khan with us," he said again in a few minutes with the same response from the crowd. Hero squirmed. "The wedding would not have been so beautiful tonight without the presence of Hero Talabani," he said louder. As the crowd applauded, a peshmerga grabbed my arm and pushed me toward the gate, which Hero was already halfway through. Our Land Cruiser was waiting outside. "My God," said Hero as we started off. "What was the man thinking? *Anyone* could have learned I was at the wedding."

"Everything is fine, Hero," her assistant Halit tried to calm her. She smoked one cigarette after another all during the thirty-minute drive to Qala Chwalan and was still tense when we sat down at the kitchen table.

"Thank you for taking me to the wedding," I said. "It was wonderful. I loved the way the Kurds danced."

"You know," Hero said, "probably everyone of them has lost at least one close family member recently, yet they continue to dance and sing and celebrate life. That's part of the strength of the Kurds. We know how to give happiness and sadness their due and no more; we joke in the face of death if we must.

"When I first decided to come here, my grandmother told me I would not last a week, that I would go mad. In England, I would cry for weeks over one person who was wounded. One of my best friends was killed in our first bombing in Kurdistan. Soon after, we were talking with a good friend by wireless and the message stopped. We thought his battery had run low, but twenty minutes later we heard that he had been killed.

"When you live in this situation, you give each emotion its due and no more. If I gave too much time to happiness, too much to sadness, I would go quite mad. If you live like this for a long time, Mariana, you too will become like the Kurds. If you don't adjust, the pressure will damage your brain."

I thought of the young men killed, the pain and grief of those left behind, the loss and deprivation suffered by the many whose homes had been destroyed. What could possibly be worth such a tremendous price? Human rights? Separation from Arabs and Turks? An independent Kurdistan?

"The Iraqi Kurds don't want or need independence," Hero answered thoughtfully. "If Iraq achieves a democracy, if we can live in our houses in peace, go to school in peace, send our husbands to work in peace—that is what we want. We have nothing against the Arabs; they were like my sisters at school in Baghdad. We must fight or be destroyed like all of the villages that you have seen. We are fighting for survival. Human rights? Maybe in a few years you won't find a human here. You must start with survival."

# 7
# BARZAN
December 1991


"Merry Christmas," I proclaimed to the surprised guard at the Sulaf Hotel late on the afternoon of December 25. His young assistant scampered down to the family section of the hotel and brought back Aisha.

"Welcome, Madame," she said, hugging me. "How was your trip to America? We have missed you so much while you were away. Mother will be delighted to see you."

The hotel had no heat or electricity now; it seemed colder inside than out. We walked downstairs to Leila's suite. A blanket hung over the door to keep the cold out. Inside Leila sat, huddled around a small oil-fueled stove. She arose, smiled, then fell into my arms laughing. "*Chon i? Bash i*? How are you? Are you well?"

"*Bash im*. I'm very well. And I haven't forgotten my Kurdish friends," I replied. "Merry Christmas!" I handed her a large box of cosmetics.

"*Gelek sipas*. Thank you very much," she said enthusiastically and hugged me again. She caressed the jars as she opened them and carefully soothed the welcome creams on her face. Leila's long black hair hung limp and had gone gray down to her neck; her face was drawn and chapped. A large safety pin fastened the dowdy beige bathrobe that she wore. She laughed nervously as she tried to make jokes about the family's circumstances.

I took four sweaters from my bag and gave them to Aisha. My daughters had carefully picked out each of them as a gift for their Kurdish sisters, whom they longed to visit in Kurdistan, I explained. "They send their best wishes and prayers that 1992 will be happier and warmer. Choose a sweater for yourself, Aisha, and give the others to Jihan, Habiba, and Tureen."

"Which one suits me, Madame?" Aisha asked, modeling each of them before deciding upon a long-lined beige one for herself.

I changed into a flannel nightgown and a robe to be warm and dressed more like my female companions. While Aisha prepared some fried potatoes and rice for dinner, Leila smiled and gently stroked my blue plush robe. She tried to talk to me, but was easily distracted, often sighing and mumbling to herself. After dinner Aisha served tea, and we talked.

"Things are not well, Madame," she told me. "Mother's legs have been swelling, and I have suffered terrible headaches. All of our winter clothes are in Baghdad; we haven't any warm clothes here. And the people in Amadiya are suffering. They have no electricity and barely enough food to stay alive. We've run out of the food we had stored. There isn't even enough rice now."

"What about the aid agencies? Aren't you receiving food from them here?"

"Nothing, Madame," Aisha said wiping her hands together emphatically to signal that nothing was left. "We get no help here at the hotel nor in Amadiya either. The peshmerga have had to leave because there is not enough food here. Only Haji has stayed."

"But there are hundreds of aid agencies working for the Kurds, Aisha."

"Father says that there is plenty of international help, but it is in the hands of other leaders; it may even be leaving the country. Perhaps it is a mistake for him to say so, but Father always speaks his mind. Father worries so much about the welfare of our people at Amadiya."

"What about his friendship with Talabani? What about help from Mam Jalal?"

"We haven't seen Talabani since you left in September, Madame. He drives through here often and doesn't even stop."

"Why, Aisha?"

"Some men are very envious of Father in Kurdistan. They envied his position with Saddam; now they envy his popularity with the people. Only Father could have delivered Amadiya during the uprising. My father stayed at Zawita and fought to protect the Kurdish people as they fled. Talabani and most of the other leaders left the country. Only my father at the Turkish border and Massoud Barzani at the Iranian border stayed. The people know that. Ali Sheban and Massoud Barzani stayed with us, for us, they always say. The people love my father and for that some of the leaders envy him and want to make him powerless. For that they hurt all of the people here in Amadiya."

The position of any leader in Kurdistan is always precarious. It depends upon his relationship with Baghdad, Teheran, Damascus, and Ankara, with other Kurdish leaders, with his people, and with major foreign powers, such as the United States and the former Soviet Union. Political strength in Kurdistan is based on an ever-changing system of alliances. Kurdish leaders are friends one day and vying against each other for advantage the next. Alliances are fragile, conspiracies legion, and betrayals the norm. While most of the peshmerga loved and admired Ali Sheban, often recalling his heroics at Zawita and referring to him as a second Salah al Din, some villagers called him a *jahsh*, literally a donkey foal, for having been a *mustashar*, a commander for the National Defense Battalion, the Kurdish militia that secured northern Iraq for Saddam. "Ali Sheban eats the poor man's bread. Massoud Barzani will return here and save us from such aghas," the head of a village near Amadiya had told me.

"Some peshmerga killed my grandfather and his brother. For that my father went to Saddam," Aisha explained. "But while he fought for Baghdad, father was always with the Kurdish people. The minute that the Gulf War was over and Haji Bush called upon the Iraqi people to rebel, Father turned against Saddam and took the cause of the Kurdish people."

It was the aghas, the tribal chiefs, the *jahsh*, urged on by the leaders of the Kurdistan National Front, who had heeded President Bush's call to rise up against Saddam in April 1991. They had had the strength and the troops to almost carry the day. Unfortunately, their peculiar feudal code kept them from fully understanding the complications of modern international politics or from comprehending that policies the victorious Western nations would adopt might not be to their advantage.

I slept in a bedroom with the girls that night, they on one bed, heaped on top of one another like a litter of puppies, and I on a bed by myself. The night grew colder and colder. Even with a sweater over my nightgown and robe, I was shivering. Aisha whimpered throughout the night. Once she woke up screaming, and her sisters were quick to comfort her. She had dreamed that the Turkish bombers, who in October had destroyed villages near Amadiya in pursuit of their own rebellious Kurds, were returning.

The Turkish government had threatened to refuse to renew the agreement which allowed Operation Provide Comfort to use Turkish air space or to enter Iraq through Turkey, which meant that the Turkish-Iraqi border might be closed on December 31. I had declared an early Christmas celebration at my Texas home in order to visit Kurdish Iraq once more before that happened. News in the States was very confusing. An academic expert had reported at the November Middle Eastern Studies Association meeting that the Turks had recently bombed the town of Barzan flat. Since only one house was standing when I had visited the Barzanis' ancestral home in July 1991, the lone survivor of the Iraqi military's rage against the renowned Kurdish tribe and family, I wanted to see what that meant. An American aid worker would take me there in the morning.

I couldn't sleep at all. I was cold, and I was worried about my friend Leila. She was accustomed to a life of comfort and elegance. Her skin was fair and fragile; she needed creams against the cold. Leila wasn't at all like Gulbihar, the princess of a Kurdish epic, who was born to run free in the mountains like a gazelle. Leila was a hothouse fairy tale princess who would have been happier back in her luxurious Baghdad home relishing tales of the heroic exploits of her warrior-husband than in sharing his discomfort and pain high in the Kurdish mountains.

The sky was a haunting navy blue that night; blue from the cold, perhaps. I could see nothing out of the window except the navy blue sky. At first light the impressive mountain next to the hotel slowly began to distinguish itself from the sky, first as a silhouette, then as a mass of gray rocks, bushes, and crevices; briefly it glowed with the bright orange reflection of the rising sun, then cooled to an unassuming tan color. I watched its metamorphoses, mesmerized by the persistence of the mountain to reveal itself. It was as if it were telling me to be cautious, but persistent, that the secrets of the Kurds would reveal themselves in time, just as the mountain had, and reminding me that the privilege of sharing these moments with the Kurds carried the responsibility of relating their story to others.

The girls were quiet as morning came. Although I hadn't slept, I wasn't tired. I put on my sweater, slacks, and a jacket and went to the door. Mr. Ali, clad in flannel pajamas, an army coat, and a fur hat, was jogging up and down the hall, keeping up his military exercise regime. Surprised and somewhat embarrassed by my early morning presence, he nevertheless gave me a big smile of recognition, then continued his jogging. I went through the blanket-covered door into the room with a stove to make tea and to write some notes. Shortly afterwards Aisha joined me and put bread on the stove for our breakfast.

"You will stay with us, Madame? How long will you be here this trip?"

"Not long, Aisha. I have work at home. Today I am going to visit reconstructions with some aid workers, but I'll be back for a day or two before I leave."

"I'm so glad, Madame. Mother is very lonely. Father is fine here and so are we. But Mother needs help. She has no nice warm clothes, no color for her hair. Madame, you thought to bring her the creams, would you also give her your blue robe? She loves it so much. All she has is the old torn one that she was wearing last night. She's very unhappy with it."

"Of course, Aisha; it's hers."

Aisha smiled and hugged me. I had barely dressed and given Aisha the robe when my ride arrived.

The day was dark and damp. Steve Saulnier, on loan from the U. S. Indian Health Service in North Dakota, spoke of his work as we drove through the gray mist. His mission was to provide clean water, a service designed to lower the death rates of infants in the area. The leg power provided by Kurdish women had made water-pumps unnecessary here, he explained. Since Kurds might not be able to maintain the pumps after Operation Provide Comfort left, the women's tradition of fetching water from a common source solved problems that otherwise might have been insurmountable.

Like most of the aid workers with whom I had visited, Steve found the Kurds to be very grateful and gentle people, who said they only wanted peace and safety. But some international workers were bothered by the violence of the area. A local political figure had been shot in front of the Military Coordination Center in Zakho several nights before, and no one, including aid workers or military officials, would help him. "He's a dead man. If the hospital were to cure him, they'd kill him there," a Kurdish driver had said, but he would not explain who wanted to kill him. The victim had been a wealthy, important Kurd, who was living in a big house with a private militia when the aid workers had first arrived in Iraq.

The day grew grayer as we approached Barzan. No longer a deserted ruin, Barzan was now populated by a large number of women in black; they were fetching water, carrying wood, or simply sitting on their haunches and talking among themselves. While aid workers rebuilt Barzan, the women were living in tents. They were the Barzani women come home to Barzan, a town that Baghdad had destroyed eight times to punish the rebellious Barzani family and tribe. Led by their legendary hero Mullah Mustafa, the Barzanis often had to flee Iraq, once going as far away as Russia, where they stayed from 1947 until 1958.

The Barzanis' many years of struggle were rewarded in 1970 with a promise of Kurdish autonomy, to be negotiated by 1974 between Mullah Mustafa and Saddam Hussein. When Saddam excluded the oil-rich Kirkuk district from the Kurdish autonomous zone, Mullah Mustafa accepted United States Secretary of State Henry Kissinger's offer of American arms to support the Shah of Iran in that country's war against Iraq. Baghdad immediately declared a unilateral autonomy decree which was not acceptable to the Kurds, and ferocious fighting broke out once more. When Iraq and Iran signed a peace treaty in Algiers in March 1975, America abruptly stopped aid to the Kurds. Kissinger's advice to the American Congress, which questioned the United States' sudden betrayal of the Kurds, was succinct: "We should never confuse covert action with missionary work."

Within days of the truce, Saddam began a brutal retaliation against the Kurds for what he considered to be their treasonous acts, a reprisal which included the use of chemical weapons. Thousands of innocent civilians were killed. Villages and towns, including Barzan, were destroyed. Many of the Barzanis fled to Iran; those who did not escape were forcibly moved to the deserts of southern Iraq. Some of the Barzanis were later relocated to Qush Tape, a concentration village near Erbil. In 1983, when officials in Baghdad decided that the Barzanis had aided an Iranian assault on the border town of Haj Omran, the Iraqi army surrounded Qush Tape and rounded up all men over the age of twelve. The men, who may have numbered as many as 10,000, were taken away and never seen again. The Barzani women, not knowing what had happened to their men, alternated between assuming them dead and hoping that they were alive and merely imprisoned. "I still listen for the barking of the dogs in the late afternoon, at the time that my son and husband would come home," one had told me.

The Barzani women had lost not only their husbands and sons, their fathers and brothers, but also their social and economic support. As Kurdish women, who are usually known as "the mother of (their son's name)" or "the daughter of (their father's name)," the Barzani women had lost their very identity. Most were forced to take menial jobs, and some of the unprotected women were reduced to prostitution. They were far from their former villages in the Barzan area and felt like strangers among the Soran and Goran, the southern Kurdish tribes. All that was left to them was their identity as Barzanis; the Barzani honor and the red turbans of their lost sons and husbands remained of utmost importance to the women.

After the advent of the Safe-haven, the women of Qush Tape met foreign visitors with framed photographs of their sons and husbands, begging for any information about them. They would perform poignant laments in which they called upon international governments and Massoud Barzani, Mullah Mustafa's son and the head of the Kurdish Democratic Party, whom they called King of Kurdistan, to open the prisons and let their men come home.

Christine Allison, a graduate student at the School of Oriental and African Studies of the University of London, worked in Iraq for six months documenting oral traditions of the Kurds. Among the works she recorded was this lament of the Barzani women.

*For the sake of God and his Prophets*
*Oh great countries and governments*
*And kingdoms, open the prison doors!*
*The young men's mothers are stricken;*
*Night and day they cry out*
*Grieving over their wounds.*

*Do not bring us clothes, no, what use are they*
*After the slaughter of the Barzanis?*
*May God soften your hearts!*
*Show us the doors of the prisons*
*So that a mother can rock her son!*

*Our children are strangers on the road;*
*Until evening they work with their hands*
*For the Soran and the Goran.*

*We want our sons to be discovered.*
*We don't know if they are abroad in Western countries*
*Or in prisons.*

*The Barzanis had great honor.*
*The Barzanis are bereft, sister!*

*Massoud, ask!*
*King of the Kurds, ask that the prison door be opened.*
*Find the Barzanis for us!*

*This is the tenth year beginning.*
*We raise the lids of our sons' boxes,*
*We lift the white clothes and the twisted red turban*
*And breathe in their smell.*

*Our wounds are inflamed, there is no cure.*
*Until word arrives about the unknown prison*
*There is no remedy for my heart.*

Sheikh Abdullah, whom I had met the previous summer when I had visited Barzan, walked through the women in black and approached us. He was a small man with light hair and a ruddy complexion. The red and white turban that signified that he was a Barzani stood out against the landscape of gray mist and women clad in black. Barzan indeed had been bombed in the autumn, he told us, and took us to the cemetery to see the bomb crater. Only one man had been killed. Another who was preparing to bathe in the river had all of his clothes blown off, but otherwise was not harmed. One afternoon soon afterwards a helicopter had brought Turkish officers to visit Sheikh Abdullah. "No Turkish airplanes have ever bombed Barzan," one had explained to him. "If we did, it was a mistake."

"I told them that my house is the only building here, and as you can see, it is not a military base."

Sheikh Abdullah's wife and daughter had been living with him at the time. His daughter left after the bombings, which had frightened her very much. "Would you consider staying with my wife Faima as a guest for a few days?" Sheikh Abdullah asked me. "She has been very lonely since our daughter left."

Did Faima really want me as a guest, I wondered. "She requested that I invite you," Sheikh Abdullah added. We arranged for Steve to pick me up two days later.

Faima and Sheikh Abdullah lived in a one-room mud house with a dirt floor. In the middle was a pot-bellied stove fueled with wood. A few pillows and mats were on the floor for sitting. The earth held the heat well, and the room was comfortably warm. Faima was obviously happy to have a visitor, although we never managed more than a perfunctory conversation. She was attended by two women servants. I smiled when I heard their names; they were called Mem and Zin, the same as the famed hero and heroine of a well-known Kurdish epic. Faima smiled back. She seemed very happy in spite of the cold and circumstances, I told Sheikh Abdullah. "Of course she is," he replied. "She is here with me." He smiled broadly.

Sheikh Abdullah spent much of the afternoon with us. Besides speaking of Barzan and the Barzanis, he would sit in the light offered by the one window and read the Qu'ran aloud and pray while we listened. The Barzanis had converted to the mystical Naqshabandi Sufi sect at the turn of the century and remained faithful to it. "Conversation with God is important to all men, but it is particularly important to the Barzanis," Sheikh Abdullah told me. Like the house and Barzan itself, his religious conviction seemed free of pretense and to the point, gentle, but not weak in any way.

"I myself am not a sheikh or a special religious man," he explained. "I was named after an important sheikh of the Barzani family." Faima was quiet and often seemed but a shadow of Sheikh Abdullah; she sat out of the light and had a profile very like his.

For dinner Sheikh Abdullah offered up a partridge from the many he had caught and put in cages. As we sat around the fire, warm and well-fed, I realized that the simple life served the Barzanis well. While there was a guest room close by, I slept in with Faima and Sheikh Abdullah in the house, which the stove had already warmed. My bed, like theirs, was a simple mat on the floor. The small mud house stayed warm, and I slept soundly throughout the night.

The next morning I bathed at the common watering place of the Barzani women; it was walled off to protect the privacy of the women while they fetched water, washed clothes and children, bathed, or sat and visited. Afterwards Sheikh Abdullah showed me more of the reconstruction at Barzan. I told him how surprised I had been to find him living alone among the ruins when I had first visited Barzan during the summer of 1991. "A Barzani must always live in Barzan," he affirmed with a smile.

When the time came to leave, Sheikh Abdullah insisted on driving me back to Amadiya himself, and Faima wanted to accompany him in his simple pickup truck. I was surprised to see her in the light. As we drove along I mentioned how very much she looked like Sheikh Abdullah.

"Of course she looks like me," he said. "After all, both of us are Barzanis."

Mr. Ali was standing on the steps of the hotel when we arrived and was not happy to see me approach in a truck driven by Sheikh Abdullah Barzani. Neither man spoke or recognized the other in any way. Sheikh Abdullah, Faima, and I said our warm goodbyes, and I thanked them for their hospitality. After they left, I addressed Mr. Ali. "I haven't joined the Barzani peshmerga," I said with a nervous smile. Mr. Ali laughed aloud. I loved my friends in Kurdistan, but kept scrupulously away from their politics, never even attempting to understand the complicated sets of alliances. My close friends always seemed to understand that.

It was snowing ferociously when I left the Sulaf the next morning. I hated to leave Leila and the girls to the mercy of the cold Kurdish winter. I hugged Aisha to me when my car arrived. "As Leila is my sister, Aisha is my daughter," I told Mr. Ali with a tear in my eye. "I shall always love and care for her as such," I promised. Mr. Ali stood proudly next to us, his grandson Mohammed in his arms. I thought that I noticed a tear in Mr. Ali's eye also.

# 8
# THE KURDISH ELECTION
May 1992

"Welcome to Kurdistan," a red-lettered sign greeted election visitors halfway across the bridge that spans the Tigris at Habur, the point where one leaves Turkey and enters Iraq. Northern Iraq, still under the control of the Kurds, was now being called Free Kurdistan. The Kurdistan Front, a coalition of eight Kurdish parties, had governed rebel-held northern Iraq remarkably well following the October 1991 collapse of peace negotiations between the Kurds and Iraqis, who subsequently had pulled completely out of the area. Since the allies' protection of the Safe-haven continued and no agreement with Baghdad was in sight, the Kurds had decided to elect a legislative assembly for the "Iraqi Kurdish Autonomous Region," and a "Leader of the Kurdistan Liberation Movement" to make internal decisions and represent them officially to the outside world. The autonomy agreement between the Kurds and Baghdad dated March 11, 1970, provided the legal underpinnings for the election. The general populace would elect one hundred members to parliament; five separate seats were reserved for the Christian minority.

Since the dislocation of many Kurds caused by the turmoil following the Gulf War made preparing polling lists impossible, Germany had sent indelible ink to dye fingers of the Kurds as they voted. Problems with the ink had caused the election to be postponed twice, but it was now set for Sunday, May 17. It was significant that the ink had cleared the United Nations embargo committee, which did not allow nonessential items to enter Iraq.

Hundreds of international election watchers, European and American governmental officials, human rights activists, journalists, and academics were arriving for the election, considered to be a milestone in the history of the Kurds. Border guards directed me to a passport office in the border control building that the Kurds had taken from the Iraqis. A tall, thin young man blessed with a shock of black hair and a black mustache and wearing a khaki uniform stood up behind his desk and greeted me. *"Chon i? Bash i?* How are you? Are you well?" He asked in Kurdish and English. "Welcome to Free Kurdistan. May we ask the purpose of your trip?"

"To photograph and celebrate Kurdistan," I wrote in a book he handed me. I planned to observe the election and visit my friend Leila and her family.

The official smiled proudly at me and inquired, "Would you like our new public relations office to arrange lodging for you?"

"Thank you but that won't be necessary. I'll be staying with the Ali Sheban family at the Sulaf Hotel near Amadiya."

His mustache fell as his smile and confidence disappeared. He turned very pale and stared at me as if in disbelief. "I don't think that is possible," he said.

"Is something wrong? Have they left Kurdistan? Has something happened to them?" Possibilities raced through my mind.

He looked down at the floor. "I am sorry to inform you that Ali Sheban and his family were all killed."

"All of them?" I gasped. "Leila? Her daughters?"

"All of them, Madame," he said, looking me sadly in the eye.

"When?" I asked.

"February, I think."

"But I just saw them in December. Who killed them?"

"No one knows. Some say Saddam;  some say other Kurds."

I thought of my conversation with Mr. Ali, when he had shared his fear for his family with me. Many times during our happy summer together I had wondered how I would feel if I learned that my Kurdish family had been killed. Now that moment was upon me, and I was numb. Although the weather was quite warm, I felt myself shiver, as if it were winter.

Something told me that it would be reckless to show too much emotion or to ask too many questions. It was not unlikely that I might be considered a part of the family whom someone was intent on killing. I bit my lip and asked, "Can you make arrangements for me to stay in Zakho?"

A young peshmerga driver took me to the newly opened Kurdish public relations office in the small town about ten miles from the border, where my lodgings, transportation, and election-day plans would be organized. Just as I arrived, Colonel Naab, commander of the allied Military Coordination Center, pulled up beside me in his jeep. "Hey, Mary Ann," he welcomed me. "Ready for a party in Dahuk?" Was I ever. I was ready for anything that didn't involve being alone. Deserting my luggage, I leapt into the jeep.

"So what's it with the American press?" a young officer stationed at Incirlik, our base in Turkey, asked. "How come U. S. journalists write pages of dirt on the personal lives of presidential candidates and don't even bother to report *this*, a major international event in which America has had a part. A *real* story is happening here, the birth of a new democracy, an election in Kurdistan!"

"It's a momentous occasion," commented Colonel Naab. "And my being replaced by a guy with more tread on him probably scares the socks off of those who wish the Kurds ill," he laughed, presenting Colonel Wilson, his replacement as commander of the allied Military Coordination Center. Naab, who had been with Operation Provide Comfort since its inception, was the last member of the original team to leave. Wilson's arrival signaled a continued American and allied commitment to the Kurds, the continuation of the Safe-haven zone in northern Iraq, and the beginning of Provide Comfort II. Tonight the Kurds would bid Colonel Naab farewell and welcome Colonel Wilson. They were extremely grateful and appreciative for the help America had given and relieved to know that the protection and relief program would persevere under Colonel Wilson's command.

Cheers went up as Naab entered the party. "Kurdistan has witnessed great events this year," said Sami Abdulrakhman, our host and the head of Kurdistan People's Democratic Party. "The Kurds' biggest uprising, the largest migration in the history of the world, our most difficult negotiations with Baghdad, and now our first democratic election, the first chance in many decades for the Kurds to choose their own leaders, to govern themselves, an opportunity brought about by the allied protection of the Kurds and the dedication and bravery of Americans like Colonel Naab. As long as there are Kurds, they will never forget our American friends and Colonel Naab."

"We Kurds have a saying," Hussein Sanjauri, another leader, explained. " 'Live short but live with dignity.' Our friends the Americans have taught us we can live long and live with dignity." With heartfelt words of appreciation, he presented Naab a plaque inscribed with  the rewritten proverb. As Haji Bush's man in Kurdistan, Naab had carved himself a niche in the hearts and history of the Kurds.

Naab expressed his appreciation, his undying love for the Kurds and Kurdistan, where he had spent a year of his life, his last as an "American peshmerga." He hoped he had made a difference to the land of his friends. "But don't underestimate what you've done for yourselves. We are very proud of you, and tomorrow is something else you will do yourselves."

To a hushed audience, Naab ventured a guess as to who would win the election. "The Kurds!" he shouted with a big grin. "So let's party!"

And we did. Hero's words came back to me, about how Kurds celebrate when in danger or in pain, her prediction that if I stayed in Kurdistan, I would become like the Kurds or else go crazy. While some of my Kurdish friends were dead, others had accomplished something worthy of celebration. With little experience governing themselves, the various groups had cooperated and arrived at a point where they were able to stage an election and choose officials to represent them in the uncertain days to come.

Before the party was over, the election was postponed again. The ink that Germany had sent was designed to mark animal carcasses, not voters, and would wash off too easily. Chemists from the University of Salahaddin had put out a call for chemicals from photographers' darkrooms and said that they would have proper ink by Monday. Tuesday, May 19, would now be election day.

"Madame," a voice behind me exclaimed. I turned around and was very surprised to see Nabil, Mr. Ali's nephew and Jihan's husband. "Have you heard what has happened?"

"I just learned," I said. "It's very sad."

"But you must not cry when you see Aisha. This has been very difficult for her."

"Aisha!" I nearly shouted. "Aisha is alive? She wasn't killed?"

"Only Mr. Ali, Leila Khan, and their youngest son. Aisha and Jihan had taken our sick baby to the doctor in Mosul, and Habib was out of the house when it happened." I was immensely relieved to know that Aisha, Jihan, and their brother Habib had been spared. Nabil's brother Asmat, one of the most respected men in the Ali Sheban family and one of the first Kurds I had met in northern Iraq, was also at the party.

"Asmat, how very nice to see you" I said softly with a smile and a tear when he approached. There was something peculiar to Kurdistan about the bittersweet sensation I was experiencing, wanting to celebrate the success of my Kurdish friends who were surviving and progressing against enormous odds while mourning those who had been killed in the struggle.

Asmat took me to the sumptuous home of Aisha's married sister Habiba, who had loved to wear gold jewelry and beautiful clothes, who had played with my lipsticks and eyeshadows by the hour. Habiba greeted me at the door all in black without a shred of makeup and fell into my arms, weeping. She fetched us tea, then sat by me, holding my hand as Leila used to do, sometimes softly crying.

I slept at Habiba's and joined Aisha the next day at Nabil and Jihan's apartment. Aisha, also in black, embraced me and sobbed like a child for the loss of her family. We cried together. The murders had occurred at their house in Dahuk, committed by poor relations in the hire, the family thought, of Saddam Hussein. Mr. Ali and his son had been shot and poor Leila repeatedly stabbed and beaten. "Mother died in the beautiful blue robe you gave her for Christmas, Madame," Aisha smiled, remembering our last happy time together. "Now we have no one. Now you are our mother."

The happy young people of last summer had entered the sad adult world of Kurdistan. The children of the brave and powerful Ali Sheban were unprotected and frightened; they were not certain that the assassins would not return.

I decided to spend election day in Suleymaniye. Many people had heard about my earlier visit to the city with Kafiya and Nazanin and welcomed me warmly. They were happy and proud of having ousted Iraqi troops from the city in October. "We have had a taste of freedom, and we can never go back to how we lived before," Xoshi, an energetic young female schoolteacher told me. "Whoever we vote for tomorrow, we are voting against the rule of Saddam Hussein."

Although voting didn't begin until eight o'clock the next morning, men and women started to form separate lines at polling stations at about five-thirty. Although both sexes were out in force, some braving lines in the hot sun for as long as eight hours in order to vote, the women of Suleymaniye, often clad in Kurdish finery and laden with flowers and cakes for election officials, were clearly the more interesting of the two. They radiated the spirited independence and determination that travelers had noted over the decades. They preferred being separated for voting, stating that it prevented men from trying to interfere with their choices. A crippled lady insisted on being carried to a polling station to vote. Hero Talabani told me later in the day that one woman voted in a wedding dress and another on the way to the hospital to have a baby. "In our troubled times, I rarely wear party dresses," a young woman in a colorful sequined dress said, "but this clearly is an occasion to celebrate."

"This is the day we have dreamed of," an older woman beamed, proudly showing her dyed finger to prove she had voted.

A conservatively dressed woman, about fifty-five years old, smiled proudly at me, held her hand high, and shouted out "Saddam! *Enchallah*! F— him!" She knew exactly what she was saying.

While women were enthusiastic about voting, they were not overly concerned about who won. "We are happy to have elections, to have a parliament. Free elections will bring peace and democracy to Kurdistan," a young woman said.

"We must take hold of our own affairs, be recognized by the West, and move forward; we cannot be viewed as pathetic refugees forever," Fatma Ahmad, an election official, told me. "A political, not a humanitarian, solution is needed for our problems."

The first task of the elected parliament, according to Dr. Atia Salihy, a gynecologist from Erbil, should be reorganizing hospitals and health clinics, left in chaos after the failed uprising. Iraqi soldiers had stripped them of necessary diagnostic, treatment, and operating equipment. As hospitals and health clinics still operated officially under Baghdad's rule, most doctors were working without pay and with far from adequate supplies.

Atia invited me to stay with her and her husband, Dr. Nuri Talabani, a noted legal scholar and cousin of Mam Jalal. Their comfortable home, which was frequented by intellectuals and politicians of every persuasion, had been particularly badly treated by Iraqi soldiers during the Kurds' flight to the borders, probably, Atia thought, because she was a doctor who had attended wounded peshmerga. She still worried about her safety. Atia took me to her clinic to meet her patients, who obviously adored her; she worried over those in marginal health from having too many babies too soon and joked with those who came to visit. And Atia taught me to drink *mastau*, a watered yogurt drink, with a wooden spoon, Kurdish style.

Atia was an educated, professional woman who patriotically served the Kurdish cause and carefully preserved Kurdish traditions. Her family, who came from Koisanjak, was said to descend from the Kurdish epic hero Emer, Lord of the Golden Hand, and his wife Gulbihar, who escaped the ruins of their legendary castle Dimdim with her two sons. I photographed Atia in her office, but for a special portrait, she preferred to be photographed at home wearing her mother's traditional Kurdish dress.

If Atia and Nuri were one of the high points of my trip, an incident that occurred while I was photographing in the countryside between Qala Chwalan and Suleymaniye was the low. I had hopped up onto a cattle truck to photograph a load of women dressed in fancy village clothes who were returning from a voting station. As I photographed them, a friend arrived with a message. The woman I was photographing clasped her head and began to cry, followed by the other women. While she was voting, two young nephews visiting her had been blown almost in two by mines. "Saddam, Saddam!" she screamed. Shaking her dyed finger at an imaginary Saddam, she began ritual lament; her companions were the chorus. I recorded the words, which she directed at me for that purpose.

*Saddam! Saddam!*
*Why do you sow mines in our fields?*
*Why do you hang our sons?*
*Why do you bulldoze our villages?*
*Why do you bury us alive?*
*We beg you, America!*
*We beg you, United Nations!*
*We beg you, God!*
*Help us and save us!*
*For our lives are destroyed*
*And we have become as beggars.*

Polls were to close at eight o'clock, but the continuing long lines persuaded officials to extend voting until midnight. Even then, not all potential voters were accommodated. Many were still waiting when the doors shut, over five hundred at one voting station. By the next afternoon, the tallies were at the regional offices and the negotiating began. The two major parties, Massoud Barzani's Kurdistan Democratic Party (KDP) and Jalal Talabani's Patriotic Union of Kurdistan (PUK) were running neck and neck, with KDP slightly ahead. No other parties had received a large enough percentage of the votes (seven percent was the threshold to seat a party) to be given a seat in the new parliament. In the contest for leader Massoud Barzani had carried the rural and more tribal Badinan and was barely ahead of Jalal Talabani, who had won in the more urban and politically liberal Soran. Neither had received fifty percent of the votes.

Although the counts were known Wednesday afternoon, it was Friday before the results were announced. PUK would take fifty seats in the new parliament, and KDP would take fifty. The Christians would have the five seats that they had been promised. Small party leaders were appeased by promises of cabinet posts. A runoff was announced between Talabani and Barzani, but their close race later was negotiated into a coalition government in which they shared power. Michael Meadowcroft of Britain's Electoral Reform Society, which had forty-six trained monitors in the field, covering 141 of the 176 election centers, declared that the election had been "a fair and free expression of the will of the Iraqi Kurdish electorate."

It was clear that the smaller parties did not have the support they thought they had. It was equally clear that Jalal Talabani and Massoud Barzani had a mandate to work together, that neither could speak alone as the voice of the Iraqi Kurdish people. Nevertheless, the Kurds had carried out their election and were ready to face the challenges ahead.

The Kurds celebrated their success in carrying out the election with singing, dancing, and rounds of gunfire into the air. They had a de facto government, a protected zone, a semi-independent state, more than any Kurds had in this century. Yet they were in a race against time and they knew it. The economy was smashed, living conditions bad, and goods scarce as the result of the two embargoes against them: an embargo from Baghdad because of their rebellion against the Iraqi government and, paradoxically, an embargo by members of the United Nations because they were part of Iraq. The people were optimistic and patient. They understood that the Iraqi government had deliberately cut off their means in order to cause massive dissatisfaction. But unless the new government could ensure basic necessities, the Kurds faced a terrible dilemma: Make peace with Saddam or face starvation, freezing, and death.

One of the first tasks of the new government would be to persuade the West to send direct technical aid for reconstruction. Aid thus far had been a dressing of the wounds but hardly a proper cure. Iranians and Turks had raised serious questions about a Kurdish rebel government in northern Iraq. By conducting the election in an orderly fashion and reaching an accommodation that was embraced enthusiastically by most, the Kurds had responded. As Colonel Naab had put it, the Kurds had won. They were getting their household in order without bringing civil war and more chaos to the region.

Within a month, Kafiya Suleman would be appointed Minister of Municipalities and Tourism, and her husband, Omar Fatah, would be off to Istanbul to buy her ministerial clothes—or as his brother Bekir called it, Kafiya's Margaret Thatcher suit. These were big changes from our summer together at Qala Chwalan, when Kafiya wore peshmerga clothes. They went with the big changes in Kurdistan. Along with other liberation fighters, Kafiya was making the switch from peshmerga camp to governmental office. Hero was one of the seven women elected to the parliament. But Hero, ever proudly a peshmerga, never changed to dresses or suits.

The change from peshmerga rule to parliamentary government went deeper than just changing clothes, however. It was time to put down the guns and address such pedestrian problems as mail, telephones, banking, and electricity—systems so totally centralized that they had completely collapsed upon the pullout of the Iraqi regime. For now, the Kurds were alive, on their feet, and anxious to take control of their own situation.

There was a new person in my life when I returned to the Badinan. Baby Leila had been born to Aisha's brother Habib and his wife

Tureen while I was away. She was perfectly beautiful, bound in her traditional Kurdish cradle. "We must marry our little Kurdish princess to my grandson Justin," I told Aisha. "She will need a brave Texas warrior with two six-guns to protect her."

Aisha smiled. "Leila, both Leilas, would like that very much, Madame."

I traveled to Turkey several times trying to help Aisha and her family escape from harm's way. As too often happens on international borders, some people's tragedies created good business for others. At that time Iraqi passports, taken when the Kurds stormed governmental offices, were sold for about twenty-five dollars; Turkish border guards sold visas to Turkey for thirty. Unscrupulous contacts charged Kurds about $1500 to assure their families would be quickly processed by refugee agencies. But Aisha and the young men of the family worried about how the women would guard their privacy in places so modern as Turkey, Europe, or America. After begging my help to rescue her family from Iraq, Aisha ultimately hesitated, then decided to stay in Kurdistan.

I visited Leila and Ali's graves on a mountain overlooking Amadiya and photographed Habib and Haji as they set up the tombstones. I tried to learn what happened to Leila and Ali. The Chief of Police at Dahuk said that a rigorous investigation had revealed that they were killed for Leila's legendary gold. Peshmerga regarded Mr. Ali as a martyr to the Kurdish cause, but the head of a village told me that the killings were arranged by local Kurds because of his former alliance with Saddam. One man reminded me of the blood feud between Mr. Ali's family and the Barzanis, and another brought up Mr. Ali's controversial friendship with Abdullah Ocalan, "Apo," the leader of the Kurdish militants in Turkey, who was at war with the leaders of the Iraqi Kurds. The facts were very complicated, and I realized that I probably would never learn the truth about the deaths. Everyone in the Badinan knew the true story of Ali and Leila, and every story was totally different. Ali and Leila had passed into Kurdish legend.

# 9
# ZAKHO AND LALISH

September 1992

The Kurds have a proverb that says, "Every valley in Kurdistan has a religion; every city, a king." While Islam became the predominant religion of the land with the repeated invasions and conquests by the Arabs and the Turks from the seventh through the twelfth centuries A.D., earlier religious beliefs had never ceased to influence pious practices in the Kurdish mountains. Early religions had included the worship of Mithra, a Persian deity identified with light and the sun, and Zoroastrianism, which stressed the struggle between good and evil. Regional traditions, including local saints, wove their way into beliefs. The isolation imposed by the high mountain ranges caused religions to develop more independently, just as the protection they offered allowed sects that were persecuted elsewhere to persist.

While its practices are sometimes eccentric, Kurdish Islam is fervent and often has strong mystical overtones. After the dissolution of the Kurdish emirates in the nineteenth century, religious men called sheikhs frequently replaced the emirs as political leaders. It was not unusual for such leaders to be affiliated with a *tariqat* or Sufi order, the most important of which were the Naqshabandi and the Qadiri. While not sheikhs themselves, Massoud Barzani and Jalal Talabani are from families associated with the brotherhoods.

Some Islamic sects in Kurdistan are not orthodox. The largest of these are the Alevis. Concentrated on the northwestern edge of Kurdistan in Turkey, they have followers among both the Kurds and the Turkomans of the region. Although Alevis, like Shi'ites, recognize the leadership of Mohammed's cousin Ali, they have little in common with the modern Shi'ites of Iran. Alevis do not perform the canonical five daily prayers, nor make the pilgrimage to Mecca. If they fast, it is not in the month of Ramadan, like other Muslims, but in Muharram, to commemorate their martyrs, and then only for twelve days.

Christians have lived in Kurdistan since earliest Christian times, and several of the congregations, including the Church of Mareyamana at Diyarbakir, claim to be the oldest Christian parishes in existence. The antiquity of the Christians of Kurdistan has intrigued Christian missionaries and other visitors to Kurdistan from the eighteenth century to the present. As one Christian relief worker explained, all sites suggested for the Garden of Eden are in Kurdistan, as is Mount Ararat, where Biblical tradition says Noah's ark landed. Furthermore, the stargazing Magi are thought to have been Zoroastrian Kurds, and Kurds in the person of Medes and Elamites were present at Pentecost. Jeremiah had prophesied that the Elamites, predecessors of the Kurds, would appear to be destroyed, but would have their fortunes restored in the End Days.

Jews lived in Kurdistan from the time of the dispersion of the ten tribes until they left Iraq en masse in the 1950's. In October 1992, I accompanied Dr. Yona Sabar, a professor of linguistics at UCLA and author of *The Folk Literature of the Kurdistani Jews*, to Kurdistan. He was returning to Zakho, his hometown, which had enjoyed a Jewish population of five thousand of the approximately twenty-five thousand Jews in Iraqi Kurdistan. Kurdistani Jews descended, tradition had it, from Jews exiled from Israel and Judea by the Assyrian kings and "lost in the land of Assyria" (Isaiah 27:13) after "the king of Assyria took Samaria, and carried Israel away unto Assyria and placed them . . . in the cities of the Medes" (II Kings 17:6).

When the Jews of Iraqi Kurdistan emigrated to Israel in 1951, Yona, a boy of twelve, was with them. Being separated from his land, he had dedicated much of his academic studies to it. He told me that he had walked the streets of Zakho many times in dreams; now he was returning to walk them in the daylight. He wanted to document the remains of the synagogue in Zakho and to record some Christian traditions in Aramaic. Once the *lingua franca* of the Persian empire and spoken throughout Syria-Palestine and Babylonia, Aramaic was superseded by Arabic following the Arabs' conquest of the area. Only in isolated Kurdistan had Aramaic survived to the present day as a spoken language, persisting among Christians and Jews there. Since the Jews had left, Kurds called the language "Christian" and scholars referred to it as "neo-Aramaic."

The Jews of Kurdistan had been pious but, being few and shut off from the rest of the world, not knowledgeable about their faith. In spite of that, they were very reverent. Ascetic practices like rising at midnight to recite devotional prayers or fasting twice weekly or more often had been common among them. Like members of other religions in Kurdistan, Jews had enjoyed visiting shrines, such as the tomb of Jonah in Ninevah and that of Daniel in Kirkuk as well as local caves supposedly visited by Elijah.

Besides urban merchants, the Jews of Kurdistan had been shepherds, farmers, weavers, rafters, and loggers, occupations that distinguished them from Jews in other places. The rafters and loggers had been centered in Yona's hometown of Zakho, situated on an island between two branches of the Khabur River, an important route from central Kurdistan to Baghdad and a major port. Their rafts were made of logs strapped together and floated on inflated sheepskins.

Yona and I explored the old synagogue at Zakho, part of which was occupied by a Kurdish family; another part was destroyed. The Jewish neighborhood of Zakho had become somewhat shabby, and of course no Jews lived there now. Yona did find some older men who remembered his father and some descendants of Jews who had married Muslims and stayed in Zakho. Many of these told Yona that they were ready to reaffirm their Judaism and join the 125,000 Kurdish Jews in Israel.

"The Kurds identify with the Jews as a persecuted race," Yona explained. Kurds had suffered from being a non-Arab minority in the Middle East, and their feelings of being left out of Muslim brotherhood had caused some of those with Jewish ancestors to want to return to Judaism and immigrate to Israel. They were disappointed that predominately Islamic states in the Middle East had rushed to the Palestinian cause, yet had totally ignored the chemical bombings of their Islamic Kurdish brothers at Halabja and other sites since 1988. "Kurds in Zakho appealed to me to carry their message to the Jews, both in Israel and in the states, to please use our power to help another besieged minority threatened with genocide."

While it was far different from the hometown Yona had left, Zakho was still a city of shepherds and farmers. Christians, still very much in evidence, had taken over the crafts that the Jews had once done, such as the weaving of cloth and making of suits. School children still whiled away afternoons on the old Ottoman bridge as Yona and his friends once had. Yona was happy with the small town, ever photographing the cows that wandered through its streets and the young boys and girls, who cried, "Hello, Mister," to any foreigner, regardless of sex or nationality.

While Yona stayed in Zakho to look for other vestiges of its Jewish past and to record neo-Aramaic conversations with Christians, I headed into the mountains to Lalish, the holy city of the Yezidis, followers of a religion peculiar to Kurdistan. It was the time of the Feast of the Assembly, a ten-day celebration commemorating the twelfth century meeting of Sheikh Adi, the religion's most important holy man, with his disciples beneath the mulberry trees at Lalish. The Yezidis would gather there to visit shrines, share food and conversation, and sing, dance, and play games.

While Sheikh Adi was an Islamic Sufi leader, the Yezidi faith includes practices common to Judaism, Christianity, Zoroastrianism, and even earlier religions, such as tree devotions and sun worship. The elements, particularly fire and water, play an important role in the religion of the Yezidis. They do not pray in mosques or temples but in private, always facing the sun. Under God the Creator, the Yezidis have seven angels, the chief of whom is Melek Taus, the peacock angel, who deals with this world. Melek Taus had refused to bow before God's creations Adam and Eve, but was later forgiven for this omission and in Yezidi lore is not considered to be the devil, as is commonly thought.

When we got to Lalish, Yezidis were arriving on foot, in cars, and aboard minibuses. As they neared their holy city, they would stop at a small footbridge and run back and forth across it, cheering with delight both ways. For the Yezidis this was the bridge between Good and Evil, Heaven and Hell. A few women dallied at a nearby tree to pick walnuts. The nuts were sacred because they contained a living substance, like the Pearl which had housed the world in the Yezidis' creation story.

Lalish, or Sheikh Adi as it was alternately called, was everything one could hope a holy city to be. It was beautiful, mysterious, and magical, a spiritual experience composed of fluted conical steeples and wide plazas, graced with springs and mulberry trees, set high in the mountains of Kurdistan. The Yezidis took off their shoes and kissed the portal of the sanctuary city as they entered. Our Yezidi hosts were friendly and warm, ever eager to be of assistance, hardly the frightening "devil worshippers" that they were sometimes described as being.

The secrecy of the Yezidis had caused many to misunderstand them. Most Yezidi texts were not written but handed down orally from father to son. An oral tradition as opposed to a written tradition kept them from the protection offered by Muslims to "people of the book," which included Christians and Jews, and had resulted in terrible massacres of Yezidis. During Saddam's reign, the Yezidi villages had been destroyed and the inhabitants transferred to collective villages where their actions could be monitored.

Only recently Pir Khadir Suleman, a member of one of the Yezidis' priestly castes, had revealed some of the Yezidi sacred texts to outsiders. Fearful that one day the Yezidis would be completely gone and remembered only as strange Kurds with big mustaches, he had transcribed some of the sacred texts and shared them with the Society of Iranian Oral Studies of the University of London, of which he was now a proud honorary member. The University of London had sent Christine Allison, a graduate student, to Dahuk for six months to work with Pir Khadir and collect texts from the Yezidi women.

Dr. Philip Kreyenbroek, a London professor and founder of the Society of Iranian Oral Studies, was joining Pir Khadir and Christine for the feast. The British scholars were happy to be in Kurdistan and able to record the traditions of the Kurds and Yezidis. Such oral literature, not sufficiently appreciated in the Middle East, was always in danger of disappearing. Of particular importance were the Sacred Hymns, which *kawals*, reciters, a special caste of Yezidis, began memorizing at a very early age. Octogenarian John Guest, a retired Connecticut banker and life-long Yezidi enthusiast, arrived with his son-in-law to document the celebration. We all felt very privileged to witness Yezidi rituals in a part of the world that had been closed to the West for decades.

Philip Kreyenbroek spent his days at Sheikh Adi studiously recording prayers and songs and taking copious notes. John Guest was up early every morning, hiking through the mountains, carefully examining every nook and cranny of Sheikh Adi to prepare a new edition of his work, *Survival Among the Kurds: A History of the Yezidis*. His son-in-law was close behind him, wielding a camcorder.

Foreign guests shared a large room with long pallets that served both as chairs and beds. We were served trays of food and tea by Faquir Murad. A diminutive man, clad in an olive-green suit piped in black, he saw to our every need. During the day we explored Yezidi ritual sites and often sat in the main open chamber, a large oblong covered room, open on one side, to take tea and converse with Yezidi pirs, sheikhs, and other holy men garbed in a variety of intriguing costumes. At night we climbed atop buildings to watch the Yezidis form circles and dance hand in hand in the moonlight.

Our first morning at Lalish we were greeted at the Sanctuary of Sheikh Adi by the Baba Chawush, the guardian of the sanctuary. The building was as large and impressive as many cathedrals. A carved black snake adorned the facade. Inside decorative cloth hangings were said to conceal holy objects, such as statues of peacocks, the symbol of Melek Taus. The tomb of Sheikh Adi, housed in a hall paneled and floored with elegant marbles, was covered with saffron-colored cloth and draped with green silk scarves. Yezidis would walk around the tomb, kiss the cloth, and tie knots in the scarves as they passed each corner. On one side of the tomb was a large cave in which holy oils were stored.

The Sanctuary of Sheikh Shems, another important shrine, is the base of a conical fluted steeple atop which is set a golden ball to reflect the first rays of the sun. The Yezidis believe that the sun brings life, is life, and that Sheikh Shems, whom they venerate, is related to the sun. Women visiting the shrine kissed the portal of Sheikh Shems' mausoleum and received a bit of sacred dirt in a handkerchief from the custodian of the shrine. They left money on the portal for the keeping of the shrine, which would be collected later by the custodian's son. The custodian spent mornings teaching the holy texts to his son; he would sit reciting them while the young man stood and repeated after him.

Many of the Yezidi ceremonies have no known explanation. The Yezidis perform certain acts because they and their fathers before them have always done so. Pir Khadir later told me many of the stories of the Yezidis and took me to their villages and grave-yards, where I saw more steepled mausoleums. Graves often are decorated with paintings of machine guns or daggers to indicate how people died and with plaits of hair that Yezidi woman have cut as part of their mourning ritual. The Yezidis have a caste system and can only marry other Yezidis of their same caste; they firmly believe in reincarnation. A good man will be born to a higher caste while a bad man may return as a monkey. "We never say that a man has died, only that he has changed his clothes," Pir Khadir told me.

The climax of the feast consisted of the sacrifice of a bull. The Yezidis were divided on the propriety of the sacrifice this year. Some of the holy men whose participation was necessary for a proper sacrifice lived in the part of northern Iraq still held by Saddam. Despite the Yezidis' pleas, the Iraqi government would not allow them to cross into the Safe-haven for the ceremonies. Those who wanted to sacrifice prevailed. They could find only a small calf, purchased with a generous donation from a German television crew that had joined us, and dragged the reluctant animal from shrine to shrine of the holy city. A colorful procession of *kawals* and musicians preceded the bull-calf. When the poor animal was taken away to be ritually killed, we all joined hands and, led by the Baba Chawush himself, danced round the mulberry trees that graced the courtyard in front of the Sanctuary of Sheikh Adi.

After a meal of fresh veal with the pirs, sheikhs, and other dignitaries in the outside meeting room, it was time for us guests to leave. The goodbyes were sad. We exchanged small presents with our hosts. I gave handkerchiefs to the young girls who had helped me and pens to the men. Faquir Murad was delighted when John Guest gave him a pair of olive-green socks to match his handsome olive-green suit.

# 10
# SALAHADDIN

October 1992

İraqi opposition leaders gathered in Ankara, Turkey, were optimistic about the coming meeting of the Iraqi National Congress to be hosted by the Kurds at the former mountain resort of Salahaddin in rebel-held northern Iraq. Saddam's excesses had made him unpopular with Arabs and Turkomans, as well as with Kurds; dissident Iraqi Kurds, Turkomans, and Arabs, Sunni and Shiite Muslims, Christians and Yezidis had begun meeting in various countries around the world even before the Persian Gulf War, determined to be poised to act in agreement should Saddam's government fall. The Iraqi National Congress at Salahaddin, the opposition's first meeting on Iraqi soil, would offer moral support to the many Iraqis still living in their country who wanted a change but were terrified to speak out. The meeting also would signal to other countries that the Iraqi opposition was organized and capable of acting together.

About half of the 174 delegates attending the meeting were traveling through Turkey, and I was invited to accompany them. We flew to Batman and boarded two buses. The ride through civil war-plagued southeastern Turkey, escorted by special forces, was painfully slow. We did not stop once, not even for water, until we reached the security of the Turkish-Iraqi border more than five hours later.

Dr. Sait Ketani, a Turkoman delegate to the conference, sat next to me. Originally from Kirkuk, Sait now lived and worked in Ankara as a forestry consultant. He had spent several years in south-eastern Turkey as a graduate student and shared entertaining tidbits about the geography and history of the area that we were driving through. After a light supper at the border, we drove another eight or nine hours nonstop to Salahaddin. We slept on the bus and awoke at about seven the next morning, as we were passing through Shaqlawa. Sait was most upset. "The forest is gone. My forest, the forest that I planted, has completely disappeared."

Sait, working directly with Saddam Hussein, had planted a forest here some twenty years ago. There were so few trees now that he could count them. "Only thirty-four shrub oaks remain out of hundreds of trees that we planted. How is this possible? *Look!* That man is carrying a root he has dug out. People are even taking the tree roots for fuel. With the root system gone, the thin topsoil will wash away with the spring rains. The erosion will be devastating."

Two days later the thirty-four trees that we had seen were gone. The only trees left standing, perhaps appropriately, were in cemeteries. Men were chopping down and women and children were carrying away the legendary arboreal splendor of Kurdistan. In Erbil, entrepreneurs were selling it. "Take a picture of that man and his wood. Title it 'Forest for sale.' Document this slaughter of the Kurdish environment," commanded Sait.

The culprit was fuel, or lack of it, occasioned by the two embargoes against the Kurds. While fuel was plentiful and cheap in most of Iraq, what little came to the Kurdish area sold for ten times the price in Baghdad. A harsh winter was coming on, and people were unable to buy fuel for their cars or for their stoves. Panicked, the Kurds attacked their trees. Iraqi authorities were quite adamant about not allowing fuel into the Kurdish area, and the U.N. embargo committee, which prohibited nonessential items from entering Iraq, had delayed fuel shipments traveling through Turkey. U.N. officials claimed that fuel would arrive for the Kurds in a few weeks.

Sait clasped his head. "In a few weeks the rains will be here, and it will be too late to plant. *Now* is planting season; it won't wait for U.N. bureaucrats. The situation is catastrophic. You have to plant crops in the right season, and it takes twenty years to grow a tree! Baghdad's malicious behavior and the U.N.'s hesitation in allowing fuel to be shipped here are provoking an ecological disaster."

Nejat Ahmed Aziz, the acting president of the parliament in Erbil, explained, "We can't tell the people, 'Don't cut the trees; you will have fuel.' We can't be responsible for them freezing to death this winter. The sad situation is that we're being protected against airplanes, but we are being killed by the embargoes."

Salahaddin was a small town, a former mountain resort about thirty miles almost straight up from the Kurdish capital of Erbil. Its many small hotels and relaxed ambiance had made it a favorite spot for meetings. Sait and other delegates were taken to "official hotels," while I was shuttled away to the "press hotel," next to Massoud Barzani's headquarters. What distinguished the press hotel from the many other small hotels in Salahaddin was that alcoholic beverages were served in the restaurant. Devout Muslims do not drink alcohol, but the less pious and non-Muslim delegates to the conference often visited our hotel "to talk with the press" and perhaps share a beer.

Samy al-Majour, a sheikh from southern Iraq, who did not drink alcohol, would sip tea with us in his flowing robes and explain that the Shi'ites of his region were "a simple people, not violent" and that they wanted to cooperate fully with those of other religious beliefs in the creation of a new democratic Iraq.

The most discussed issue at the conference was the idea of uniting the various ethnic and religious groups into a democratic federated Iraq, a federal state that would guarantee minority rights and the freedom of cultural expression. Both Kurdistan and Iraq were mosaics of ethnic groups. While Sunni Arabs controlled Iraq, no group constituted a majority in the country. Kurds and Arabs, Turkomans and Assyrian Christians, Sunni and Shi'ite Muslims had to find a way to get along.

The principle of federalism was new to the Middle East, where governments had been highly centralized since the region's countries were created at the end of the Ottoman Empire in the 1920's. The centralized systems had led to terrible abuses of minorities, not only in Iraq, but throughout the region. The Iraqi opposition's idea of creating a federation would seem to some to be a revolutionary and Western-imposed notion much like the concept of nationhood that had spawned the division of the area into Western-style countries. Federalism and minority rights in Iraq might prove upsetting to the country's neighbors, especially Turkey, Syria, and Iran, who were concerned about their own Kurdish minorities.

The Turkomans were an important minority in Kurdistan. The large percentage of ethnic Turks in northern Iraq was one of the reasons that Turkey had never given up its claim to the area, known as the Vilayet of Mosul during Ottoman times. Sait introduced me to his boyhood friend Sanaan Ahmad Agha, the head of the Turkoman Brotherhood in Erbil, to learn from him Turkoman views on the new Kurdish parliament and on the opposition meeting in Salahaddin.

An ancestor's sword from the Crusades and a bust of his father proudly adorned Sanaan's office, two stories above one of the main plazas of Erbil. Sanaan's family had fought for their people since before the Crusades, but they had renounced arms to work towards harmony in a multicultural society. "The Turkomans, Kurds, and Christians are like brothers living in the same area; we depend on one another," Sanaan asserted.

The Turkomans wanted peace, security, and cultural rights, to be partners with Kurds, Christians, and Arabs in a federated, democratic Iraq. Sanaan firmly believed that the former Vilayet of Mosul with its population of Kurds, Turkomans, and Christians would have become an independent Kurdistan or part of Turkey had it not been for what he called "British intrigues." If a federated Iraq, in which the cultural rights of Turkomans, Kurds, and Christians were guaranteed, was not possible to achieve, then the Turkoman community felt that both of the previous options were still open. If the majority of the people of northern Iraq agreed, the Turkomans would accept the area becoming part of Turkey or an independent Kurdistan.

"We are Iraqi citizens first, then inhabitants of Kurdistan, and last of all Turkomans—unless there is trouble. Then we are first of all Turkomans."

Kafiya Suleman, now Madame Minister of Municipalities and Tourism, saw the problem of minority rights as crucial and difficult, especially in a part of the world that knew neither democracy nor such rights. Kafiya was glad to be where she was now, glad that the Kurds had arrived at this plateau, as she called it, and was optimistic about the democratic movements throughout the world.

"When we were fighting, we were fighting for today," she said. "I have worked in every aspect of the fight, and now I am enjoying the ground we have won. But we cannot say we have finished; we must continue working. And the fight is not only for equality and democracy in Kurdistan, but in all nations."

Women delegates to the conference offered various paths for arriving at a democratic Iraq. Nada Al-Samerae, a striking twenty-six-year old Arab optometrist from London, dressed Islamic style in a fashionable long black coat and a scarf that totally covered her hair. She was returning to Iraq for the first time since she was a baby. Nada blamed the suffering of Iraqi Kurds and Arabs alike on the governments that had put Saddam in power and given him arms—the Persian Gulf countries along with the allies. None of the major powers had reprimanded him for using chemical weapons against the Kurds and other Iraqis at Halabja, Nada said. "Only five years ago we were frightened to say we were against Saddam. Now the very people who backed Saddam Hussein are supporting us."

An elegant, articulate Kurdish woman, Thuria Mohammed Abdullah called herself Mrs. Mustafa to honor her recently deceased husband, whom she had replaced as a delegate to the conference. She was happy to see Kurds meeting with Arabs, molding ideas about the future of Iraq before Saddam's collapse. Mrs. Mustafa was firm on the need to guarantee minority rights. "Our Arab brothers in the opposition must understand what the Kurds want now, before the opposition comes to power. And what we want is federalism."

Nada challenged Mrs. Mustafa, fearing that federalism in Iraq would not be an acceptable solution to Iran, Syria, and Turkey because of their own problems with minorities.

"Iraq belongs to the Iraqi people," countered Mrs. Mustafa emphatically. "Kurds, Arabs, Turkomans, and Christians alike, not to Syria or Turkey or Iran. The Kurds must demand federalism as an ideal now, before the opposition comes to power. The Kurdish area of Iraq must connect with the center, but not be smothered by it."

For all of their differences, the conference representatives set up a democratic system by which to solve their problems, and at a press conference on the evening of October 31, Iraqi National Congress spokesman Hoyshar Zebari proclaimed the conference a success. Arabs, Kurds, and Turkomans, Christians, Yezidis, Sunni and Shi'ite Muslims had agreed on a moderate political program, elected and authorized the moves of a president and three-person executive council, and declared that the future Iraqi government would be a pluralistic, federated parliamentary democracy. Businessman and banker Dr. Ahmad Chalabi would be president of the Iraqi National Congress; former Ba'athist General Hasan al-Naquib, Kurdish leader Massoud Barzani, and Shi'ite clergyman Sheikh Mohammed Salih Bahr al-Uloom would make up the presidential council. Renouncing a Republic of Fear in favor of a Republic of Tolerance, Chalabi announced that a democratic, federal government would be the first step to national unity in Iraq.

Just as the congress was beginning to rejoice in its success and take its message to the world, news arrived that Turkish troops had marched into northern Iraq and right through the streets of Zakho, supposedly in pursuit of Kurdish militants from their own country. But Turkish soldiers had killed some Iraqi Kurdish pesh-merga, an act that Barzani, on behalf both of the congress and of the Kurds, condemned soundly. And then Iranian aircraft began flying over Iraqi Kurdistan.

On my way out of Iraq, I stayed a night with Hero and Jalal Talabani at their new headquarters in Erbil. Given their knowledge and insight, perhaps they could help me sort out what I had seen: the deforestation, the opposition meeting, the Turkish incursion. Jalal, ever the politician, was very optimistic: Turkey would withdraw; the West and the Iraqi citizens would support the decisions of the opposition meeting; the PKK would calm down; and the new American administration would support the Kurds. After he left, Hero had another viewpoint.

"Don't be fooled by appearances of calm. Our situation is more dangerous than ever. The Turkish invasion, the Iranian flights over our area, the fuel shortage, the increase in refugees from Kirkuk are bad signs. People are frightened. Families are selling their furniture and clothes to keep their children in school, but many have had to take them out. They have money either for food or for school bus fare. Most people are jobless. And Saddam is waiting for his chance."

Later Jalal said, "I am certain Hero explained further everything that I told you."

"On the contrary, she disagreed with your every point."

Jalal laughed. "You see, Mariana, we are democratic in Kurdistan, even in my own home."

# 11
# CHRISTMAS IN KURDISTAN
December 1992

The Kurdish parliament and the Iraqi opposition did not work miracles. Christmas was near, and Saddam was still in power in Baghdad. He had responded to the Kurds' efforts to govern themselves and make independent contact with the outside world by tightening the embargo from Baghdad and encouraging terrorism against the Kurds and those helping them. The foreign ministers of Turkey, Iran, and Syria had opposed federalism for Iraq, which they feared might be the first step toward dismembering the country. Some members of the Turkish parliament thought both the elections and the opposition activities were part of an attempt by America and Great Britain to rule northern Iraq and wanted to halt Operation Provide Comfort altogether. Turkey had never relinquished its claim to northern Iraq (the former Vilayet of Mosul) and did not want any other countries controlling it. Relief workers in Kurdish Iraq complained that U.N. security was inadequate and that U.N.-negotiated money exchanges were leaving over ninety percent of aid money in the hands of Baghdad money changers.

I returned to the Kurdish area with cameraman/director Christian Jacks, a friend since the Gulf War in Diyarbakir, to examine the effect of these setbacks on the Kurds and to document how they were coping during the winter. My friend Hoyshar met us at the border a few days before Christmas and took us to the PUK guest house in Zakho, a two-story former residence with terrazzo floors and painted plaster walls. He led us into a warm room with comfortable furnishings and oriental carpets, where Bekir Fatah, Kafiya's brother-in-law, met us.

"How are Kafiya and Omar?" I asked.

"Kafiya is working hard at her ministerial job. Omar is retired, home cooking and washing dishes. I wish that I could find my wife a job." Bekir smiled, pouring us generous glasses of cognac. "Let's turn on BBC and see if the Iraqi army has taken our governmental offices in Erbil yet," Bekir playfully suggested, but he really tuned his radio to the BBC to get an update. As Hero had once said, Kurds sometimes joked about the things that frightened them most.

Life wasn't easy now in Kurdistan. Winter was upon us, fuel was low, and food was scarce. I asked Bekir what it would take to break the Kurds and send them back to Saddam.

"If people start to die from starvation or from cold. If illness sets in, the game may all be over." Bekir was realistic. The Kurds were tough but not invincible. He arranged a Land Cruiser and a driver for Christian and me to travel across the Kurdish area and see for ourselves.

The roads were almost empty the next morning. A few days before we arrived, a sixteen-truck convoy returning to Turkey had been blown up. One driver had noticed a weird sound in his truck and stopped the entire convoy. From the side of a hill, they had watched the trucks blow up one by one. Turkish drivers were no longer enthusiastic about delivering relief to Iraq.

Christian and I stopped just outside Dahuk to photograph the remaining trucks there. Drivers made extra money by trafficking in cheap gasoline from Baghdad to Turkey. Since the embargo did not affect gasoline tanks under the load, the wooden beds of Turkish trucks were cut off to make them as high off the ground as possible, and large homemade gasoline tanks were strapped beneath them. The homemade gasoline tanks and the strangely shaped trucks were folk art tributes to the embargo. They often spilled oil and gasoline on the highway, however, causing terrible wrecks, often followed by fires, in southeastern Turkey.

While fuel was in short supply and priced out of reason for most Kurds, there were plenty of places to buy it. Every few yards we passed a Kurd with a stack of brightly colored five-gallon gasoline containers. "If an extraterrestrial being landed here, he would think Kurdistan was a land of gasoline station owners," Christian commented. When we stopped for fuel, our driver Naryman would sniff the gasoline, carefully choosing the right vintage for his Land Cruiser. Some gasoline entrepreneurs sold fuel that could ruin a car.

We photographed around Dahuk in the afternoon and were surprised to see an armed man at the cemetery. "I'm guarding the trees," he told us. Even the trees in cemeteries were not safe now. We videotaped the Bishop of Dahuk saying late afternoon mass at the Chaldean Catholic Church, then joined a Christian friend, David, for a drink at the bar of a popular hotel. David, who worked with the U.N. refugee program, had told me last summer that he would never leave Kurdistan as a refugee. Now his family was en route to Canada, and he would join them soon. I wondered what had changed his mind. We had just sat down and ordered tea when the smell of gunpowder filled the room and several men hurried out. We followed them and passed a fire truck speeding toward the hotel. We lost David in the confusion, but we had learned in a dramatic fashion the situation that had influenced his decision to leave northern Iraq.

Later, at her home, Leila's daughter Aisha explained the continued flight of people from Kurdistan. Although allied planes kept Saddam from attacking the Kurds, he had begun to terrorize them. Small bombs were set off constantly in the market place, and people were afraid to go out of their houses. With fuel scarce and the worst of winter yet to come, the Kurds were frantic. Saddam's tactics had rendered the new government powerless. "Better we should never have had the uprising. And I am not the only Kurd who thinks that." The price of the uprising had been high indeed for Aisha, since she had lost her parents, but with cold and hunger threatening now, it might seem high to others too.

Since the Gulf War, the roads had become a barometer for the well-being of Kurdistan. When things were going well, they were full of traffic. This Christmas we nearly had the road to ourselves. All along the road to Erbil, Kurds were hacking at the few miserable trees they had left and carrying away their remains. The gasoline sellers near Dahuk gave way to firewood entrepreneurs as we approached Erbil, and shepherds herding their sheep were armed.

On my last trip, we had crossed the Great Zab on a new bridge constructed by a European relief agency, but since that time members of the Serchi tribe, angry because the bridge had disrupted their profitable ferry service, had blown it up. The rather ingenious ferries were working again; they consisted of rafts atop floating oil barrels, pulled by cables connected to tractors on each side of the river.

Fuel was low, electricity sporadic, and food scarce in Erbil, where the parliament was hosting a conference to promote the idea of development in Kurdistan. "We grow a surplus of tomatoes, but tomato sauce has to be brought in from Turkey," Hussein Sanjauri, Assistant Minister of Economic Development, told Kurds and Europeans who were attending. "We have abundant sunflowers, but we must be sent sunflower oil as well. Machines given us to extract the oil have been held by the embargo committee in Turkey. It would take so little for us to become self-sufficient. Perhaps the truth is that our neighbors don't want us on our feet."

The parliament building in Erbil was about eight stories high, an old Iraqi governmental structure complete with the marble facing and sumptuous decor one expects of official structures. Peshmerga friends from former trips were there, many wearing Western-style suits appropriate to their new task. Mam Rustum missed living with his troops, but he recognized that the challenge to Kurdistan was political, that parliament was the fighting front now, and he wanted to be here. He also was working to organize the peshmerga into a regular Kurdish army. But for now, with all of the work there remained to be done at the capital, lack of heating and electricity caused parliament to have to recess.

Since Erbil was closing down, Christian and I decided to travel to Suleymaniye. We arrived on December 23, just as night was starting to fall. A few bonfires lit the otherwise totally dark streets. I stayed with Nazanin, and Christian stayed next door with her brother and his family. We all came together in Nazanin's living room to talk. The mahogany and velvet chairs, the oriental carpet, and the large china cabinet full of mementos of happier times were familiar even in the dark. The dark and the cold that caused us all to huddle on the floor near an oil stove was a new experience.

"Tomorrow is Christmas Eve, Nazanin," I said. "Christmas is an important holiday for the West and for the Christian minority in Kurdistan. It is the day when we believe Saint Nicholas will bring us presents and make our wishes come true. What is your Christmas wish this year? Food? Central heating? Airline tickets to London?"

"Kirkuk!" the adults answered almost in unison, naming the oil-rich and always hotly contested region and its capital, which were still in Iraqi hands.

"Kirkuk? It's freezing, you have no fuel, you're short on food, and you want to fight? You want to take Kirkuk?"

"Absolutely," answered Nazanin, smiling. Her brother shook his head in agreement. "Kirkuk is our home. There is no town more Kurdish than Kirkuk; Kirkuk is Kurdistan. If we must die, we will die for Kirkuk."

Kirkuk is an oil-rich area where Kurdish land borders that of the Arabs. As is typical in border lands, its population is mixed. Turkomans dominated Kirkuk city for many years and Kurds the countryside of the region; Arabs were sprinkled throughout the area. In the 1970's, legendary Kurdish leader Mullah Mustafa Barzani forged an agreement with Baghdad to grant Kurdistan autonomy and won on almost every point except the inclusion of Kirkuk in the autonomous zone. To obtain Kirkuk, he went back to war, risked and lost everything, and fled to America, a sick and broken man. Since then Saddam has made Kirkuk central to Iraq's Arabization process, removing Kurds and Turkomans from the Kirkuk area by force and replacing them with Arabs. This disruption displaced many Kurds and Turkomans, who now lived in make-shift camps in the Kurdish territory and desperately wanted to return to their ancestral home.

Suppose this Christmas season that Baghdad offered the Kurds the chance to live in peace, to rule themselves, to keep all of the territory they had won. The price, however, would be renouncing their right to Kirkuk. Could they give up Kirkuk?

"Never!" The idea was outrageous to them.

Christian and I sat on the floor in the cold and the dark, listening to small bombs exploding outside, and were amazed. Nazanin took a candle into the other room and brought back books and maps, which she proceeded to open and spread out on the floor.

Kurdistan may never have been a country, but it has always been more than a myth. Kurdistan is usually defined as "the land of the Kurds" or "where the Kurds live." Customarily, it has meant the lands where the Kurds predominate. Kurdistan's boundaries and size are invariably debated. While Turks, Arabs, and Persians minimize the extent of Kurdistan, Kurds portray it as quite large. Nazanin's maps were among the most generous to the Kurds.

"Kurdistan goes from the Mediterranean Sea to the Black Sea to the Caspian Sea," she explained, pointing to one of the maps. "This is the land of our people, the land of the Kurds. And this is Kirkuk." She pointed to a city on the map. "Kirkuk is our home, the spiritual center of Kurdistan. Kirkuk must always belong to us. We will sacrifice all that we have—everything, our lives, our homes—for Kirkuk."

"This is schoolteacher stuff. I bet those kids don't buy it," Christian whispered to me, motioning toward Nazanin's two teenage nephews, who were sitting apart from us on a sofa, looking somewhat bored. "I bet they'd rather be in London or Manhattan."

He confirmed that over tea the next morning. "I went up to the kids' room last night. They showed me maps of Australia, maps of South America, maps of Europe—maps of Alaska, for God's sake. They want to go anywhere but Kirkuk. They really want out of here now that they can't go to Baghdad anymore. They say there is action in Baghdad." Christian poked me in the ribs. "Fast women, fun, nightlife. While their politicians buy condos in London and their kids plan Saturday nights in Baghdad, the brave schoolteachers of Suleymaniye will have to charge Kirkuk alone."

The next day Nazanin took us to the women's teachers' college in Suleymaniye where she worked. An attractive young woman in a white blouse and navy jumper burst into tears as she spoke to us. Students were sharing a few battered books; pencils and notebooks were scarce.  In most homes siblings fought for the one oil lamp to study at night. Students who bore chemical scars from the tragedy they had endured during the destruction at Halabja were now being overcome by small but continuing day-to-day difficulties. They were frightened that they wouldn't be able to continue their education. "If we stay in this situation, we shall start to go backwards. We are becoming so depressed. But when someone like you cares enough to visit, we become proud and think that we deserve to live."

The Iraqi government refused to send Kurdish language schoolbooks warehoused in Baghdad to the area, and 80,000 books sent by *France Liberté* were held up by the embargo committee in Turkey. UNICEF failed to deliver promised pencils, paper, and notebooks. "It is one step forward, one step back," Nazanin said.

Mines were drawn on the blackboard at a UNICEF-funded school that prepared men to teach in reconstructed villages. Curriculum included mine identification and safety, first aid, and psychology courses to help teachers work with children who had experienced the destruction of their homes and villages and, in some cases, the killing of members of their families. UNICEF had erected 420 prefabricated school buildings in the villages, and *Equilibre* and Danish Church Aid were building desks from scrap lumber—wooden crates that they begged from other relief agencies.

At the "Kurdish Bastille," the former Iraqi Security building from which Kurds had freed political prisoners in a grisly hand-to-hand battle in 1991, we photographed some of the thousands of Kurds and Turkomans displaced from Kirkuk who now made the complex their home. Children as well as adults residing there tended to the task of living well with pathetically few resources. Women baked bread while their daughters carried dishes and clothes to the one water distribution rack to wash. Several women had set up a cottage industry and were making large pottery jars for grain storage.

After our visit to the schools and displaced person camp, Nazanin took us to the workshop of *Zhinan*, the Women's Union of Kurdistan, an organization created by Hero and Kafiya when they were peshmerga in the mountains. For all that they had suffered, Kurdish women resisted becoming victims. Through Zhinan relatively well-off women helped their more distressed sisters, especially those who had lost brothers and husbands, to rebuild their shattered lives. Volunteers raised money for Zhinan by weaving distinctive fabrics and hand crafting Suleymaniye party dresses to sell to visitors; they taught the bereft simple skills to keep them from becoming beggars. At the workshop, about fifty women were busy at sewing machines, turning out baby clothes a relief agency had ordered. "One sewing machine can support an entire village," Nazanin told us proudly.

After videotaping the schools, camp and Zhinan's workshop, Christian and I went shopping. Our first stop was the fuel oil merchants lining the streets. We taped Nazanin and our driver Naryman bargaining for fuel oil and in the process bought enough to keep our houses warm for a few days. We then stuffed Naryman's pockets with dinar and sent him to find some chickens and cognac. Rice and tomatoes would not suffice for a Christmas Eve dinner.

We didn't sing carols, but we did eat well and warmly. "You know, I never miss family and friends at Christmas. I find a working holiday like this much more satisfying," Christian confessed as we passed around the platter of chicken a second time. I suddenly realized that I did too.

Colored lights twinkled bravely on a tree next to the altar, powered by their own generator, in the otherwise dark church on Christmas morning. Gasoline lanterns cast strange shadows and stranger colors on the ceremonies. Ancient Aramaic echoed throughout the church as parishioners chanted the age-old nativity text. The bishop, dressed in festive red and white holiday vestments, was nearly bald and had a long white beard. He looked tired and worried. Three cameramen from Kurdish television stood directly in front of his pulpit, showing concern for the Christian minority by taping their commemoration of the birth of Jesus, the Prince of Peace. *Shalama*, the bishop begged in his sermon, *shalama*. "Peace be with you. Blessed be the peace makers. Lamb of God, who takes away the sins of the world, grant us thy peace." And just in case the Good Lord didn't deliver, twenty-three Kurdish guards stood in the entrance court of the church, Kalashnikovs on the ready.

About two hundred fifty shivering Christians, clutching their coats tight around them and holding their prayer books with gloved-hands, squeezed into the small church. Somber men sat on pews in the front of the church; devout women and wiggling children filled the back rows and the balcony, which creaked beneath their weight. The hall was adorned with simple renditions of madonnas and saints and the back wall covered with a velvet painting of Jesus as the Good Shepherd, a role well understood in pastoral Kurdistan. In the women's section hung a portrait of the Virgin Mary. She was a young Mary, holding the Babe, but she was drawn and haggard, a strange mixture of the Virgin Mother and the Dolorosa, or the bereaved Mary. She was Mary as a refugee mother.

Few people were on the bitterly cold streets of Suleymaniye the next day. Men huddled around stoves at kebab stands and small fires they had built on the street. Land Cruisers full of peshmerga drove aimlessly around traffic circles in which naive statues commemorating the feats of Kurdish martyrs had replaced monuments to Saddam. We left the city and traveled to Qala Chwalan to visit the peshmerga training school. Instruction was based on the West Point manual, which had been translated into Kurdish. The young men had shaved heads; they marched smartly and stood for dinner, which they had five minutes to consume. Mam Rustum and friends would see that the trainees broke the two-hour lunch and the thirty-minute tea habit.

Nazanin, Christian, Naryman, and I drove to Penjwin, the destroyed town high in the mountains on the Iranian border where I had spent happy summer days in 1991 with Bekir Haji Safir and his family. On the outskirts a small crowd of men were standing beside their Land Cruisers and mules. Most were probably smugglers returning from a trip over the mountains to Iran. They gathered around a monument to the peshmerga, and bought kebabs from men who had set up booths to service the travelers. A man with a team of three mules spoke to us. "Smuggling is the last traditional profession that pays well in Kurdistan," he said.

A schoolhouse in Penjwin had large holes from artillery attacks, and children, still wearing gloves, coats, hats, and scarves, read and recited their lessons in the freezing, nearly dark classrooms. Numerous victims of mines and small bombs moaned mindlessly in the nearby hospital, which hadn't anywhere near enough painkillers or medicine to treat the wounded. One hapless baby, swollen with burns covering three-fourths of his body, whimpered constantly. "He threw a bomb he thought was a toy into the family fireplace," a doctor told us. "Most of the family died in the fire."

On the thirtieth we decided to drive to Zakho via the road through Barzan; snow had closed the better road through Aqra for several days. We drove to Salahaddin and past Shaqlawa. When we got to our turnoff, the checkpoint guard said that no vehicles had come through all day. The Barzan road was probably closed also. We elected to drive on for about an hour and to spend the night at Diyana, a village near Rawanduz. Night was just falling as we pulled into the small town and learned that the nearby hotels had closed. British Save the Children saved the day, putting us up in their office for the evening.

The next morning, Christian and I shared coffee and a lively discussion with Simon Mollison, the head of British Save the Children, a maverick relief worker who was expanding his operation in northern Iraq even as his less enterprising colleagues were having to leave. Rather than have his efforts frustrated by money changers and Iraqi-backed terrorists, Mollison openly dealt across the Iranian border. "When we needed livestock to replenish the flocks that had been destroyed here, we didn't buy goats from the Iraqi government. We ordered the animals from local Kurds and didn't question their origin. We paid a fraction of what Baghdad would have charged us."

"But your humanitarian operation here looks like a fort in a Western movie," Christian challenged. "Is this a measure of your importance, an example of Iraqi 'gunmen chic'?"

Simon smiled. "Like it or not, we are worth attacking for those who would like to stop our work here. Saddam is offering fifty thousand dinar, about three thousand dollars, for any Westerner killed. That's tempting to some."

"There has been so much trouble with fuel, schoolbooks, simple machinery. Could the aid program totally collapse?" I asked.

"It nearly did. The acute winter emergency got it going again, but only with great difficulty. Baghdad has done everything in its power to stop relief work. Some small agencies have been willing to come in and work cross-border illegally, outside of the control of the Iraqi government, but the big players—the U.N. and so on—have not. Perhaps that will change now. Western governments seem fed up with the U.N.'s respect for the Iraqi government."

"Is the Kurdish experiment in nation-building doomed?"

"Perhaps. But the alternative, the Iraqi army coming back, is unthinkable. A massive refugee crisis would occur, and everyone fears that. We've worked hard to forget the Kurds, and suddenly we can't. There's still a lot of good will toward the Kurds in the West."

"Why should the West help the Kurds at this point?"

"Because it's very easy, it's cost effective, and because we can actually stop a disaster. That's not always the case."

"Do we rebuild a nation to accomplish that? Do we create an independent Kurdistan or a federated Iraq?" Christian asked

"We don't have to do anything like that. We merely improve the ability of this besieged area to be self-sufficient during the period that it's besieged."

"Kurdish parliament? Is it a Western institution imposed upon a feudal system?" Christian continued.

"The feudal tradition is only part of the picture. Like many modern states, Kurdistan has several systems that coexist. It's a growth process."

"How long will this stand off last?"

"My optimism goes up and down. We've moved a lot this year, mostly backwards. But perceptions in the West are changing."

"Like?"

"A year ago we couldn't do anything separate from Baghdad, which terrorized both Kurds and aid workers and cheated the people out of millions in currency exchanges. Now there is hope that Western governments will address the issue of massive destruction by the Iraqi regime and help the Kurds to rebuild the infrastructure. With just a little bit of outside help, Kurdistan could be self-sufficient. But certain interests think that Kurdistan should not be self-sufficient at this time. The Turks don't want it; the Arabs don't want it; the Persians don't want it. Ultimately the U.N. responds to them and so do the U.S. and Britain, for fear they will stand accused of coming back to colonize. Just hanging on might be the best thing that could happen to the Kurds at this time. For now, uncertainty is hope."

I wanted to stay in Diyana and celebrate New Year's Eve with Save the Children at nearby Guli Ali Bek, a small park where rushing water broke dramatically through the Kurdish mountains. Christian was firm. The Americans would probably host a party in Zakho—with food and drinks and electricity and heat. From there, we could drive across the border to Turkey and dine at the Istanbul Hilton before New Year's Day was over. The food and heat convinced me.

The road was empty at first, but after Aqra, aid trucks began to arrive from the Turkish border. The Turks had recovered their confidence and were driving again. A light snow started, but the roads did not seem to be icing. Truck traffic increased, snow piled up, and lanes narrowed. We had been slowed down, but we hoped to cross the mountains and be in Dahuk by nightfall, then continue down the better road to Zakho. But high in the mountains, about an hour from Dahuk, trucks and cars came to a complete standstill. Traffic and snow had closed the road. Temperatures were dropping, and night was falling.

My friend Hoyshar and an Australian photographer whom he was guiding appeared at my window. Their Land Cruiser had been in a small wreck and had broken a window. We wrapped them in coats and blankets, and I zipped myself into my down sleeping bag and tried to sleep, wanting to forget that it was New Year's Eve and I was hungry. As midnight drew near, I thought of the party at Guli Ali Bek. I thought of food and wine and all the warm parties taking place elsewhere. At midnight on the dot Christian miraculously produced a can of tuna fish and a hidden flask with five generous shots of cognac. "Happy New Year!" he proclaimed.

"Hey! This is even better than Christmas," I replied, and I was only half kidding.

# 12
# CİZRE
March 1993

Often in defiance of orders forbidding displays of their culture, the Kurds continue to celebrate their March 21 *Newroz*, the Kurdish New Year. Newroz commemorates the triumph of Kawa, a hero of Kurdish legend, over a tyrant who fed on the brains of young Kurds. Its bonfires attest to the Kurds' will to persist culturally and politically in countries where they are persecuted. In the 1920s, remembering the losses the Ottoman Empire had suffered because of Arab, Greek, and Serb nationalism, Ataturk legislated Kurds and their language out of existence in the newly formed Republic of Turkey. Not protected by international conventions which applied to Turkey's non-Muslim minorities—Greeks, Armenians, and Jews—Kurds became known as "mountain Turks," Turks who, in the seclusion of their mountain habitats, had forgotten their language. Frustrated at being denied their ethnic identity and culture, Turkey's Kurds began a series of revolts against governmental authority.

In the 1980's, the Kurds of southeastern Turkey found themselves caught in a particularly grisly conflict between the *Partia Karkaris Kurdistan* (Kurdistan Workers' Party), the PKK, which called for recognition of all Kurdish rights and a federated Turkey, and the Turkish government, which claimed such demands jeopardized the integrity of the state. Kurds were harassed or killed by Turkish forces if they refused to join the village guards, a Kurdish paramilitary force that supplemented troops fighting the PKK, and by the guerrillas if they refused aid to the rebels. At first, most Kurds felt trapped between two equally malignant forces; as Turkish governmental measures to curb rebellion became increasingly oppressive and were applied to the general Kurdish population, their support for the PKK grew. During Newroz of 1990, Kurds in Diyarbakir, Silopi, Nuysaybin, and Cizre took to the streets, tearing Turkish flags and crying, "*Biji Kurdistan*! Long live Kurdistan!" That action escalated into a broad-based rebellion which European journalists called "Turkey's dirty miniwar" between Turks and the Kurds of Turkey.

In 1992, to the horror of on-looking humanitarian workers, journalists, and human-rights activists, Newroz became a bloodbath in Kurdish Turkey; over a hundred people were killed, fifty of them in Cizre alone. During the next year the number of dead in the continuing war between Kurds and Turks rose to nine thousand, the number of Kurdish villages destroyed to 263. Over four hundred "unsolved murders," death-squad-type assassinations, occurred; many victims were doctors, health workers, and human-rights activists—nineteen were journalists trying to cover the Kurdish story.

"Please tell our story," the twelve-year-old son of a human-rights attorney begged me in the oil production town of Batman. "I am afraid for my parents. Batman is a 'kill and go free' town. We have laws to protect us from small things, but not from the killings."

The Turkish government blamed Hizbollah, the Islamic Party of God, for the murders, but Kurds accused the *kontregerilla*, an allegedly Turkish government-sponsored death squad.

The Ankara-appointed chief of police in Cizre joined official Turkey in denying the existence of the government's death squad. "*Kontregerilla yok!*" he told me emphatically, squarely blaming the killings on the PKK fighters and Hizbollah.

The popularly elected devout Islamic mayor of Cizre had a different idea. "Hizbollah means Party of God, but Turkish Hizbollah is not made up of God-fearing Muslims nor of fanatic Islamic backers of the Iranian government. Turkish Hizbollah is a pack of killers unleashed by the Turkish government, and people here are very frightened. When Prime Minister Demirel says, 'The patience of the Turkish people is running out,' he is sending a signal to those on the right that they will have a free reign to kill Kurds."

As Newroz 1993 approached, Abdullah Ocalan, "Apo," the Syrian-based leader of Turkey's Kurdish militants, declared a cease-fire; Turkish Prime Minister Suleyman Demirel responded with a promise to allow Kurds to celebrate Newroz and to keep southeastern Turkey open for travel during the holiday.

"*Newroz piroz be! Newroz piroz be!*" the young shoe-shine boys outside of the Kadooglu Hotel in Cizre shouted. As I climbed the steps to the entrance, they cried, "Hello, how are you, auntie?" They knew me from previous trips and welcomed me with a term of endearment and respect.

Jeeps filled with armed Turkish soldiers zipped around town, splashing mud. "Cocky Turks!" complained one European journalist, as we walked through the town. "Armed to the teeth, wouldn't you know?" added another, pointing out an armored Panzer manned by young men with automatic weapons. In fact, the Turkish soldiers were little more than boys, perhaps frightened, but maintaining a stern demeanor in keeping with their military mission. Dressed in camouflage, they looked like my son and his friends ready for a hunt in South Texas.

People in the marketplace were preoccupied and aloof. Their places of business had been badly damaged in last year's *Newroz* fray. The growing numbers of Turkish soldiers and European press, along with memories of Newroz past, must have made them apprehensive. A few battered, deserted houses evidenced the shelling to which Cizre's neighborhoods had been subjected. Residents had repaired their homes as best they could, often making use of yellow Turkish vegetable oil cans, which were becoming an important building material in all of Kurdistan. Women baked bread, knitted, and continued with their embroidery and sewing, seemingly ignoring the arriving soldiers and journalists, usually harbingers of ill in the small city. School-age children jumped in front of my camera making the victory sign, but they seemed more in need of attention than intent on spreading the revolutionary word.

While Cizre's streets were quiet, the Kadooglu Hotel was bursting with activity by dinnertime as people continued to arrive. Sheri Laizer, a New Zealand author whose *Into Kurdistan: Frontiers Under Fire* described her experiences in Kurdish Turkey, invited me to her room to talk in private. As we sipped glasses of *raki*, Turkey's anise liqueur, a percussion concert familiar to Cizre commenced in the street below her balcony: *Ak-ak-ak-ak-ak-ak,* the Cizre anthem, the march of the AK-47's. Tracer fire lit up the sky, people scrambled in the hall outside our door, and the hotel suddenly went dark.

"Are you girls quite all right?" the BBC producer who had accompanied Sheri inquired from outside our door. "Don't do anything foolish or dangerous. Perhaps it would be safer if you joined the other journalists in the hallway."

Sheri and I were more interested in the pattern of the gunfire than concerned by it. "There's something strange about the firefight," I observed. "The rhythm is wrong; the shots are too even, too constant."

"I think it's a show for new press and human rights workers," Sheri said. "The fire is going straight up and down the main street in front of the hotel, not veering one way or the other." A young journalist from a Turkish agency made a great show of trying to photograph the fire. He entered the dark room on his elbows and knees, crawled between Sheri and me, jumped up suddenly at the balcony to take a picture, then crawled quickly back out of the room. "Wouldn't it be great if that young Turk used his machismo to write a credible story about what's really happening in Cizre?" Sheri asked.

As soon as the shooting stopped and the lights came back on, two vans full of people arrived. They got out, unloaded their bags, and talked nervously among themselves. They were human-rights workers, parliamentary deputies, and Kurdish enthusiasts from Finland, one of the delegations arranged by Medico International, an organization formed by German doctors. Upset by the horror they witnessed in southeastern Turkey during Newroz in 1992, German physicians had set up an organization to encourage and help European journalists, politicians, and humanitarian advisors attend Newroz 1993. The members of Medico International hoped that a European presence at the Newroz celebration would curtail somewhat the violence between Turks and Kurds.

Later, Turkish parliamentary deputies from the Kurdish party arrived and promised to escort Finns and press to Sirnak, a high-spirited town of Kurdish activists that had been nearly obliterated in last year's fighting. Turks said that the PKK had attacked Sirnak, but Kurdish residents maintained that Turkish artillery had destroyed their homes. Most of the 35,000 who once lived in Sirnak had fled. The remains of the small city and the few people left there were heavily guarded, and governmental roadblocks rarely let cars pass. Our trip to Sirnak would test Demirel's promise to allow all Kurds to celebrate Newroz and to keep southeastern Turkey open for travel.

I had only just lay down to sleep when a new noise began. *Bum-de-de-bum-bum! Bum-de-de-bum-bum!* It was the Ramadan drummer. These were the last nights of Ramadan. In Turkey and northern Iraq, drummers walked the streets in the wee hours of the morning to awaken the faithful so that they would have time for a good breakfast before the fast began again. *Bum-de-de-bum-bum! Bum-de-de-bum-bum! Ak-ak-ak-ak-ak-ak-ak-ak! Bum-de-de-bum-bum! Bum-de-de-bum-bum! Ak-ak-ak-ak-pow!* The Ramadan drummer didn't stop for the skirmishes; the skirmishes didn't stop for the Ramadan drummer. As lights started going on in homes in Cizre so that the many faithful here could enjoy a Ramadan breakfast, I finally got to sleep.

Morning revealed damage to several homes in Cizre. Mehmet, a bearded man of about eighty, had no idea why his house had been targeted. He leaned back precariously in a straight-backed chair and talked with friends gathered in the muddy patio of his house. He seemed neither overly concerned nor surprised by the destruction wrought by last night's fighting. Some women drew water at the well in the patio, while others baked bread; they continued about their daily business as if nothing extraordinary had happened. Still other women, interested in the growing crowd of journalists, peered down from the second story of the house through a broken window pane; they looked like paintings of Renaissance madonnas framed as they were in the arched window. Bullet holes placed almost symmetrically around the window added a macabre touch to the scene.

Fifteen or so cars and vans lined up for the drive to Sirnak at about nine-thirty. Many of the groups gathered for the trip had attempted to travel to the troubled town the previous day, but, despite Demirel's promise to keep southeastern Turkey open for travellers during the Newroz holiday, they had been denied entrance into the area. Journalists were excited by the opportunity to see Sirnak for themselves, and human-rights observers were anxious to leave someone there to witness any problems during the celebration. Soldiers at the roadblock stopped the caravan; I didn't understand what they were saying among themselves. "They're not inclined to let these unclean, infidel journalists and human rights observers proceed," Sheri explained. Angered by the insults, a Kurdish deputy got out of his car and began to argue loudly with the soldiers. Two intrepid photographers jumped out of their cars to photograph; a dozen colleagues and four television crews quickly followed. Finding themselves surrounded by cameras, the soldiers tensed, talked hurriedly among themselves, then quieted down. After a call to their superiors, they allowed the caravan to continue.

As we approached Sirnak, snow came down cold and hard. Through the flurries, the small city appeared to be but another quiet, picturesque Kurdish village. Earth-toned adobe houses rose one on top of the other much like those of Indian pueblos in the American southwest; the roof of a lower one served as a courtyard for the house above. Kurdish school children greeted us as we got out of our cars at the entrance to the town and walked with us through an arch embellished with a well-known quotation of Ataturk: "Happy is he who calls himself a Turk."

The streets of Sirnak were dismal. Many buildings had been destroyed or severely damaged in the fierce fighting that had plagued the city, and most homes bore the wounds of mortars and machine guns. I broke loose from the group as quickly as I could and headed for the home of some women I had met on a previous visit. My friends were surprised to see me, but delighted to have a visitor. I brought them portraits of their family, and they gave me a welcome hot cup of tea, baked sweets, and a much appreciated warm pair of hand-crocheted socks.

When I trudged back to the main part of town, I found my Kurdish driver standing below Ataturk's words. He did not look happy. Everyone else had driven back to Cizre, and we had been left alone. "I didn't know what to do. Some of the journalists hid in homes to pass Newroz here, and I thought perhaps you were with them. I couldn't decide whether to leave or to stay."

"*Newroz piroz be!*" I said.

He smiled. "*Newroz piroz be!*" he answered.

Cizre seemed an open-air cathedral filled with the thick, gray smoke of sacred fires when we returned. One could hardly doubt that these mystical fires lit on the eve of Newroz had somehow united Kurds since primordial times. My driver begged off accompanying me to the fires. "The special forces would take my license number and deal with me later," he said.

Young boys and girls, their heads wrapped securely with scarves to hide their identities, were rolling tires into a pile in the middle of the street near the hotel and lighting them. Daring young men raced toward the flames and jumped over them as their comrades defiantly flashed the victory sign.

I joined friends walking to the nearby neighborhoods. Women and girls had built a large fire on a vacant lot overlooking Cizre, and we could see the city's low skyline through the smoke. I was impressed by these proud, defiant women who stood by their fire, but Sheri was more interested in a loud group of children about a hundred yards away. The youngsters, ranging in age from about four to ten years old, were waving an over-sized Kurdish flag of red, yellow, and green material, and fervently chanting:

> *The Flag of the Kurds, raise the Flag,*
> *The Flag is our religion and our faith.*
> *Long live Kurdistan! Long live the Kurds!*
> *We die again and again for our flag.*

The white teeth of the zealous children gleamed eerily through the smoke, and their tense little faces were distorted by the passion of the moment. Even possessing such a flag was considered treason in Turkey, and people demonstrating with a Kurdish flag could be punished as traitors to the country. No adults were with them, and I wondered what motivated the children.

"Kurdish nationalism is growing. It's always more evident at Newroz," Sheri told me.

"Even in children?"

"Especially in the young. The PKK guerrillas get younger and younger; many teenage girls have joined them. It's a sad situation, but the Kurds of Turkey have nothing left to lose. When the older men are killed, a family often sends its children to fight for the PKK."

The next morning was very wet and cold. Tanks and Panzers lined the road near the hotel. Women in the neighborhoods had donned traditional Kurdish dresses and were singing and dancing in the street. One end of town exuded the song and color of a fair and fiesta; the other, the macho bravado of hunting season. While Kurdish girls tried their new dance steps, Turkish tank gunners were commandeering the weapons of their mechanical behemoths and posing for photographers. A group of little girls about eight years old gathered to sing in the main street. As they joined arms to begin Kurdish folkdances, one of the soldiers turned the large gun of his tank in their direction, and they ran screaming down a side street.

A crowd of about four hundred people gathered in a muddy square surrounded by houses in the nearby Cudi neighborhood; they were singing and waving a large Kurdish flag. I walked up an outside staircase to the roof of a house, stopping midway to wave at women sitting in the patio below. On the roof women were chanting and clapping. One showed me a weaving she had made of the proscribed combination of colors—red, yellow, and green. She flashed me a smile and the victory sign. Her white scarf covered all of her hair and face except for her eyes.

Suddenly, a strange, terrible mechanical growl stilled the demonstration. Women on the square screamed, and men ran down side streets as fast as they could. A Panzer turned the corner, sped onto the square, jerked, growled, and commenced to terrorize the women, who gathered their children about them. The Panzer raced around the square, growling, jerking, and threatening the women until, as if tired from the chase, it came to rest just under the roof on which I was photographing. Although the young men had sweaters pulled up to their eyes, ski caps pulled down, and wore sunglasses, I recognized them as young men I had photographed on the square, the ones who had reminded me of my son and his friends back home in Texas.

The Panzer went back into action, driving from door to door, menacing the women and their children. As it stopped on the other side of the square, women peered around the corner of their house to see what it was doing. A soldier opened its top and looked around. Automatic weapon in hand, he jumped down, followed by two more men, and began to chase one lone, terrified Kurdish man through the square. While women screamed at them, the three soldiers grabbed him by his arms and legs and dragged the struggling man toward the

Panzer. Women followed fast behind them, scolding the soldiers and shaking their fists. Undaunted, the soldiers pulled the man, who was still fighting, into the Panzer. The door closed, and the angry Panzer charged the women. It roared from house to house while some of the women hurled insults at the mechanical beast. It rested again, and soldiers once more came to the top.

Suddenly, without warning, the young men opened fire with their automatic weapons. *Whoosh! Ak-ak-ak-ak-ak-ak-ak-ak*! The noise and wind coupled with my own reflex reaction to the fire knocked me off of my feet. Stunned, I looked around to see Turkish journalists huddled up against a barrier wall on the roof. On the roof across the way Sheri and a television crew were also down. Peering over the edge of the roof I saw that only the Kurdish women below were still on their feet, their children gathered at their skirts, face to face with the assailants. I remembered that fifty people, including a journalist, had been killed in a similar incident the previous *Newroz* in Cizre. Blood rushed to my face, and I felt very warm. Anger and adrenaline overcame me. How dare those young men misbehave like that, acting in a way that could ignite an explosive situation and bring unnecessary grief to Kurd and Turk alike? What irresponsible commander had allowed these impetuous youths out on their own, driving a Panzer and armed with automatic weapons? What more mischief might they effect with all witnesses on the ground? The fury of the moment and concern for the Kurdish women and children overcame any fear that I might have had for my own safety; I jumped to my feet and began to photograph.

The Turkish photographers and television crews were back on their feet in a second. All was quiet except for the clicking of the cameras. Then the soldiers opened fire again. *Whoosh! Ak-ak-ak-ak-ak-ak-ak*! The wind and noise of their weapons was augmented by the sound of breaking glass. Down on my back again I realized that the soldiers had shot out the windows of the house on which we were standing. Then, as quickly as it had arrived, the Panzer growled, jerked, and drove away. I read later in a Turkish report that they had received a message from their commander to stop firing and return to their base immediately.

I got up and dusted off my clothes. To my dismay, my only skirt was completely covered with mud. To break the tension and divert one young photographer who looked very frightened, I exclaimed in mock dismay. "Oh, no, I've mud on my new skirt!"

"Oh, no, the lady's dirtied her skirt," Turkish photographers teased in unison and began to photograph me trying to clean my filthy skirt.

"And I bet these women never invite us back for tea," I said, pointing at the bullet holes below us. Everyone laughed.

The next problem for photographers was protecting film from authorities, who might not want the story out. Turkish photographers were rolling up their pants and putting the exposed film into their socks, then covering them with their pants' legs. About that time a writer from a Turkish wire service walked up the stairs to ask me about the incident, and I persuaded him to take my film back to the hotel for me. "Are you sure that the bullet holes in the house are from this attack?" he asked me.

"Absolutely," I answered.

"Did the Kurds provoke the attack?"

"Like how?"

"Did they wave a Kurdish flag or chant Kurdish slogans?"

"Flag-waving and slogan-shouting are reasons to open fire at women and children?" I asked earnestly.

My Turkish friend grimaced as if in pain, but he didn't answer me.

Always more than bizarre, the Kadooglu Hotel was like the bird house at the zoo when we returned—loud, chaotic, and absurd. The police chief gave a press conference, followed by press conferences by deputies, human rights professionals, and everyone else who thought that his opinions on Newroz and Cizre were urgently important. The noise and confusion were more annoying than being shot at. Crescendo, bravado, fortissimo—the symphony called Cizre was out of hand.

I wanted to return to Iraq, but someone said that the border was closed. I drove to Diyarbakir, took the next flight to Istanbul, and as much as I had wanted to stay in Istanbul for the Sheker Bayram, the Sugar Feast, I boarded the first available flight to London.

# 13
# VAN

April 1993

"*H*osgeldeniz! Welcome!" Turkish Prime Minister Suleyman Demirel stopped in his tracks on the red carpet and greeted me. "How long have you been in Turkey this trip? Why haven't you come to Ankara to visit me?" It was not unusual for Demirel to speak to me, but this exuberant welcome at the Van airport seemed odd.

"Tourist season this year will be better than ever," Demirel beamed at other nearby photographers. He was in Van to open the tourist season, raise the spirits of depressed area businessmen, and gain favorable publicity in the West. He was exuberantly happy to have at least one Western journalist respond to the many invitations that had been sent out.

"Mr. Demirel, don't you think that announcing a tourist season is a bit premature? Don't you think that encouraging tourism in a war zone might be irresponsible on the part of the Turkish government?" I inquired.

"Nonsense," he said, still smiling at photographers about their task, "Turkey is very safe; the reported dangers are the usual untrue exaggerations by the European press. There is no place in Turkey where you cannot travel and photograph as you wish. You have my word on that. And to better serve tourists, we are making Van airport a port of entry into Turkey."

Burhan Kartal, one of Van's most knowledgeable carpet merchants, was at the airport to meet me. During my first trip to Van in May 1990, he had introduced me to the world of the wondrous and varied carpets traded in Van. For long hours we had traveled vicariously through the Van-Hakkarri area as Mr. Burhan flipped through piles of rugs representing the tribes of the Herkes, Jalalis, Goyans, and the dozen or so Hartushi clans. He had proudly pointed out photographs of his own carpets and comments attributed to him in William Eagleton's *An Introduction to Kurdish Rugs and Other Weaving*, the authoritative book on the subject, but cautioned me that these pieces could not be called "Kurdish" in Turkey. In 1990 Van they were referred to simply as Anatolian or Caucasian.

Mr. Burhan's father was among the notables hosting Demirel. As was often the case with Kurdish families in Turkey, the Kartals' political allegiances were mixed. Several kinsmen were deputies in the Turkish parliament, but some were members of Demirel's party and others of the predominately Kurdish party. Mr. Burhan discreetly kept his political preferences to himself.

"We hope that Demirel is right and that the coming tourist season will be very good in Van," he told me as we drove to a nearby neighborhood where weavers lived. The violence of the continuing war between the PKK and Turkish troops had caused them to flee their traditional villages for the safety of Van city.

While the gray cement block houses looked very different from the earth-toned adobes and stone houses of Kurdish villages, the families of the weavers had managed to adapt them architecturally to their needs. Several had built village-style corrals in front of their houses to keep small herds of dark-haired sheep and goats. Many inhabitants of the neighborhood were related and from similar clans and tribes. Most continued to wear their traditional dress, even though such clothing, along with Kurdish language, song, and other demonstrations of cultural identity, were strongly discouraged by the Turkish government.

Whatever beauty was destroyed by removing the looms and women from their land was restored by the exquisite afternoon light. The Van sun produces a piercing white light like no other on earth. Some say it is caused by the reflection off of gigantic Lake Van, seven times the size of Lake Geneva; others say it comes from an interaction of the sunlight with the multitude of white mountain peaks that surround the lake. As the sun rays hit the deep wine and brilliant chartreuse of the women's dresses, the colors wove a spell of mystery and pleasure that was distinctly Kurdish.

The women's hands moved swiftly and precisely across the looms; young girls crawled into their laps and traced the movements of their mothers' hands as they carefully crafted the rugs for which the area is famous. Piroz, one of the women whom I photographed, was a widow with seven children. She was from the Alan clan, one of the clans that made up the Hartushi tribe, and came from a village in the Hakkarri mountains south of Lake Van. With the help of her daughter-in-law, Piroz could weave a *kilim* in about thirty days. Creating the piece would take more time if she also dyed and spun the yarn, which, after having abandoned the practice for years, she was beginning to do again.

Most of the fine flat-woven rugs known as "Van kilims" are made by tribes from the Hakkarri mountains south of Van and take their trade name from the Van market-place. Since clans and tribes share similar designs, rugs are classified by structure and quality. Local names for carpets often come from life-situations of the weavers. One Jalali *cicim,* a weft-wrap flatweave, is called a "divorce your wife" kilim, because the failure of a woman to master the complicated weaving technique is said to give her husband grounds for divorce. According to Mr. Burhan there were about 10,000 looms serving the Van market, each of which could produce five or six rugs a year. Ten to twenty per cent of these would be of highest quality, made of yarn spun and dyed by the weavers.

After photographing the weavers, I joined the women of the Kartal family, who surprised me with a night out in a Turkish bath, which they had reserved. "I have closed the bath for my guest and my family," Mr. Burhan proclaimed. "That is quite a feat in Turkey." And quite a show of caring hospitality. While dousing myself with bowls of warm water, surrounded by young girls scampering through the bath and older women seriously removing dead skin from their arms and legs, I thought about my strange welcome at the Van airport. I suspected that tourists and rug-buyers were going to be more scarce here this year than Suleyman Demirel would like to admit.

The next morning I photographed children playing beneath Van castle, a ruin set atop an impressive ridge known as the Rock of Van. The castle is one of several in the area said to have been the work of Uruatians, skilled builders who had ruled the area until they were displaced by the Medes, precursors to the Kurds, and the Armenians, some 2,500 years ago. On the other side of the Rock grass grew between the few stones that remained of the old city of Van. Van is a chiaroscuro town, made up of brilliant light and dark tragedy, the unforgettable light produced by the combination of natural wonders and the terrible mystery of the disappearance of the Armenians.

In the first century B.C. the Armenians had founded a kingdom at Van and in A.D. 280 became the first nation to officially adopt Christianity. Although overcome by invading Muslims in the seventh century, Armenians remained the majority in Van until the beginning of the twentieth century. What happened then is shrouded in mystery and debated with passion by Turks and Armenians alike. Turks claimed that Armenians were traitors who, while Turks were fighting in Russia in 1914, had burned Van and fled. One Ottoman official of the time had suggested that the Russians enticed the Kurds to kill the Armenians, then blamed the Turks. Surviving Armenians said that the Turks had set fire to their families' houses and brutally slaughtered their relations. All that is certain is that hundreds of thousands of Armenians disappeared from what was once known as the Armenian plain.

New Van is homely; it has no vistas of Lake Van nor of the exquisite ruined Armenian churches that dot the area. Van has turned its back both on its wondrous nature and its troubling past. Nevertheless, the shops that stock exotic rugs, the animated coffee houses, and the bustling small hotels on the main street can make Van a merry place to while away a summer evening. This trip seemed confined to sites away from the business district. Mr. Burhan now kept his rugs at a flat near his home. His shop was closed for repairs, he said.

"Remodeling?" I inquired.

"We had a small fire," he explained.

Although Mr. Burhan was somewhat reluctant to take me there, I wanted to visit the main street of Van. I was stunned at what I saw. Mr. Burhan's shop was completely gutted; only the exterior walls stood. The popular beer hall next door was also gone. The hotel I had stayed in was closed. The once lively street was quiet.

The authorities had said that Hizbollah had set the fire at the tavern, and it had spread to Mr. Burhan's shop. "Perhaps some devout Muslims were offended because liquor was drunk there," Mr. Burhan offered. Or perhaps it was set because the man who owned the beer hall was known to be a politically active Kurd.

I remembered Demirel's promise of safe travel and decided to go from Van directly to the Iraqi border, rather than take the safer route through Istanbul and Diyarbakir. No driver from Van would take me, but a driver in Silopi, who had earned his stripes driving press through difficult routes in the southeast, agreed to fetch me. We left Van at six in the morning. The sight of the sun rising over the snow-covered peaks and lake was marred by numerous tanks and troops. Van looked like an occupied country. On the outskirts of Bitlis, I photographed families going about chores in front of a picturesque row of houses. A hundred yards up the road we were stopped.

"Why were you photographing military installations?" a uniformed man asked. "What permissions do you have?"

"I am a tourist," I smiled politely.

"We'll have to take your film."

I handed him a bag of exposed film with no argument. "If I can only photograph Lake Van and castles, Van weaving, and Suleyman Demirel promoting tourism, then I won't photograph in Turkey anymore. And neither will any other photographer with a shred of integrity. So let's get down to the business of destroying this film right now, young man." The firm motherly approach always worked on men of a certain age. This one was about twenty-seven, the same age as my son.

The soldier's mouth dropped open. He looked confused and called a superior on his hand-held radio. About ten minutes later, a Turkish officer appeared, took one glance at me, and frowned at the guard. "There seems to have been a mistake. You may proceed, and we will give you an escort."

"I don't want an escort."

"It's dangerous here."

"Your prime minister says not."

"But we only stopped you for your own protection."

"You wanted to take my film for my protection?"

He gave up arguing with me and waved us on. We stopped to photograph tobacco sellers in Bitlis and men plowing their fields in the nearby countryside, then turned onto the dusty roads over the mountains to Sirnak, where I wanted to visit friends. The mountain villages were separated from the rest of Turkey by dreadful roads and had no schools, no health centers, and no transportation. Women sitting in front of their homes cleaning and grinding corn were frightened by our car. A young soldier, totally taken aback as we approached Sirnak, radioed for assistance.

"And what do you think you're doing here?" The Sirnak chief of police recognized me.

"I'm a tourist," I smiled.

"Tourists aren't allowed to visit here in the southeast. Turkey can be a very dangerous country, as well you know. Tourists should never stray from their groups in this country."

"Your prime minister Mr. Demirel told me it was quite safe to tour eastern Turkey."

"Well, Mr. Demirel has given you some very bad advice."

"Mr. Demirel said I could photograph anywhere."

"Mr. Demirel was misinformed."

"Then you don't suggest tourists visit eastern Turkey?"

"God, no!" The chief was on the verge of losing control. But his frustration and anger seemed directed not at me, but at Demirel, whom the military had twice ousted from the prime minister's post and whom they very often appeared to hold in contempt. The police provided us with an escort through Sirnak and sent us on our way to the Iraqi border. The Turkish officials refused to give my taxi driver permission to drive into Iraq at such a late hour, so I walked across the bridge and hitched a ride with peshmerga to the PUK guest house in Zakho, glad to be back in the relative safety of Iraq.

# 14
# BENASLAWA

April 1993

For my last photographic tour through northern Iraq, PUK public relations director Bekir Fatah arranged for a car, driver, and two translators "for just in case."

"My friend Younis is in training," explained Aziz, a slight young man in his late twenties. He had an impressive aquiline nose, dark effusive eyebrows, and wore Western-cut trousers and a blue blazer. Until last month, Aziz had taught English in secondary schools, a job he left reluctantly when his savings ran low. Teachers at his school had received no pay for six months, and the PUK translating job paid relatively well. His friend Younis, a tall chemical engineer from Baghdad with rosy cheeks and an easy smile, had been drafted into Iraq's chemical corps during the Gulf War, deserted, and headed to the Kurdistan of his parents. After working free for many months in a Sayid Sadik hospital, Younis came to Zakho in search of a translating job.

"I had an apartment, furniture, and a fiancée in Baghdad before the war and uprising. Now I have nothing," he lamented. "But maybe my luck will change."

"We Kurds hate guns and violence. Kurdistan should be the Switzerland of the Middle East," the young men told me almost in unison, as they stashed Kalashnikovs beneath the seats of our Land Cruiser. While a far cry from the I'm-married-to-my-gun peshmerga I had known my first summer in Kurdistan, my pacifist translators were out of the car, guns drawn, whenever I photographed. It was clear that Kurdistan was not so safe as it had been on other trips and that the new young men in my life were more than translators.

The minute we were on the road our driver, Samde, a tall, lanky young man blessed with curly black hair and mischievous light eyes, floorboarded the Land Cruiser and burst into exuberant song. Our young Orpheus belted out tragic tales of lovers parted by war, of a young girl who wanted to be an apple and travel to battle in the pocket of her friend. He sang of mountains and freedom, of bloody battles and peshmerga heroics, of hope and romance, of despair and death. Kurdish life with all of its complexities and nuances unfolded in vivid quatrains as we bounced along. Samde's resounding voice, fortunately, was better than the shock absorbers on his Land Cruiser.

Samde invited us to stay with his family in Benaslawa, a *mujamma'a,* a concentration village, near Erbil. Saddam built these unusually grim concrete villages starting in the mid-1970's, when he began his destruction of Kurdistan. As self-sufficient Kurdish villages were bulldozed and dynamited, their land was given to Arabs and the inhabitants moved to collective villages, where their movements and activities could be closely supervised. The collective villages were usually placed away from water or arable fields to make their inhabitants totally dependent on the Iraqis who guarded them. The residents needed permits to leave the concentration villages, even for a day's shopping in Erbil. Those who left without permission were gunned down by patrol helicopters. Most of the families of Benaslawa were victims of the Arabization that had taken place in the oil-rich area of Kirkuk.

Benaslawa sat in the middle of a dusty plain, looking like a huge cinder block punctuated by a few dirt streets. It was nothing like the warm adobe villages set among trees and streams that the Kurds had called home. We drove straight to the home of Younis' friend, Ozer. Behind the stark cinder block wall was a pleasant patio covered by grapevines, where Ozer and his sister welcomed us. After serving us tea in the main room, his sister retired to the kitchen to make bread. She sat on the floor of the kitchen, patting out round bread patties to bake in her small electric toaster oven, made of a yellow Turkish vegetable oil can into which an electric element, smuggled from Iran, had been inserted, an ingenious answer to the shortage of appliances occasioned by the two embargoes.

Younis and Ozer sat cross-legged on a long, narrow rug next to the door, while Aziz and I sat on a similar rug across from them. Aziz meticulously translated as Ozer carefully recited, detail by detail, the story of his surrender to the Iraqis and subsequent escape from a death camp. He spoke slowly and precisely, almost as if reciting an epic, and always inserted the time and day. When the Kurds' watches were taken and they were locked in dark places, the hour, learned by stolen glances at timepieces that some miraculously had hidden, became very important. Ozer's ability to pay strict attention to such seemingly meaningless minutiae may have saved his life.

Ozer was born in the village of Tajeb in 1963. Like many young Kurds, he was drafted into, then deserted, the Iraqi army. He hid out in various Kurdish villages before settling in Jafan. When the Iraqi troops destroyed that village, Ozer fled to Khidir Rehan, which in April 1988 fell victim to the terrible *Al-Anfal.*

Al-Anfal (literally "the spoils of war"), the military operation designed to solve "the Kurdish problem," derived its code name from the title of a *sura*, a chapter, of the Qu'ran which pertained to wars against infidels, and during the Anfal the Iraqi government allowed soldiers to loot, rape and murder Kurds. Hardly a religious measure, the Anfal included the displacement, disappearance, and murder of hundreds of thousands of Kurds, most of whom were Sunni Muslims, and the destruction of many village mosques by the Iraqi Corps of Engineers. The infamous campaign was carried out under the command of Saddam's cousin Ali Hasan al-Majid, called Ali Chemical because of the brutal gassing he had ordered on Kurdish towns and villages. In its publication *Genocide in Iraq: The Anfal Campaign Against the Kurds*, The Middle East Watch, which had been gathering information for a genocide case against Iraq in the International Court of Justice at The Hague, described the Anfal as "a deliberate attempt on the part of the government of Saddam Hussein to destroy, through mass murder, part of Iraq's Kurdish minority." Between March and August of 1988, over 2,000 Kurdish villages were destroyed and hundreds of thousands of Kurds were rounded up, sorted out, and dispatched to their deaths, prison, or resettlement camps. Baghdad officials kept detailed records of the complicated eradication process and often broadcast its progress on government radio and television.

The Anfal consisted of a series of eight military offensives in six distinct areas of Kurdistan carried out between February 23 and September 6, 1988. The third Anfal, in which Ozer was caught, took place in the Germain, the warm land, a hilly plain in the southern-most part of Iraqi Kurdistan, not far from Kirkuk. Iraqi troops burned, pillaged, and bulldozed hundreds of Kurdish villages, then engaged in a series of pincer movements to herd fleeing civilians toward designated collection points.

Khidir Rehan fell on April 10. Believing the Iraqi army's promise of amnesty, most Kurds of the area surrendered. Ozer gave himself up to Qasem Agha, a *mustashar* from Koisanjak. "Qasem Agha promised that the government would do nothing bad to us, that we would only be moved." After routine questioning and sorting by villages, the Kurds were transferred to the police station at Qader Karam, where they were videotaped with Ali Chemical himself.

Over nine hours in a three-day period Ozer told us point by point how the Kurds were separated, sorted, numbered, and often dispatched to their deaths by firing squad. Ozer's ability to absorb and accurately remember small details probably saved him. Despite massive confusion, he never lost his sense of time and place, and because of that was able to assault his captors and escape through the open pits of Kurdish graves. Killing and disposing of so many Kurds was a logistical problem on which the Iraqi government kept copious notes. These notes, which corroborated Ozer's story, were later captured and turned over to human-rights organizations, who were using them to substantiate their case against the Iraqi regime.

After hearing the first few hours of Ozer's story, we went to Samde's house for dinner. Kak Ahmad, a man in his mid-fifties clad in peshmerga clothes and a turban, sat against a wall, propped majestically on pillows atop a narrow Kurdish carpet. Two friends of his vintage sat one on each side of him. The three men were loudly singing the glories of Kurdistan. When they stopped to take tea, about half an hour after we arrived, Kak Ahmad told us his story. He had lost his legs from an infection after having his toenails pulled out while being tortured. Kak Ahmad laughed, joked, and inserted entertaining asides as he spoke, his Kalashnikov in his lap. There was not a trace of regret for the way he had lived nor of surprise at the results, no sign of self-pity. He had been a hard-living, hard-fighting peshmerga, and he accepted the price that came with that choice. "Talabani and I are very close," he smiled, showing a recent photograph with the PUK leader. "He is a good man. I fought for him many times." After the long trip and an evening filled with stories and song, we all slept soundly on pillows on the floor of Kak Ahmad's house.

The first person up the next morning was seven-year-old Kawser, who gulped down breakfast like schoolchildren all over the world, fussed with her hair, put on her boots, and was ready to go when her best friend arrived. They joined a river of Kurdish children, their schoolbags on their backs, hurrying to make their first class on time.

When the gates of Lana primary school opened, a mass of waiting children rushed in, happy and excited to be at school even though the buildings had no water and most of the doors and windows were broken. Since there were few desks, most students sat on bookbags their mothers had made. Within fifteen minutes of the bell, the children were loudly reciting their lessons throughout the school building. "The children are enthusiastic and eager to learn," their principal told us. "What few problems they have stem from poverty."

A man from the destroyed village of Tubza who lived close to the school summed up the plight of the residents of the *mujamma'a*. "We never had enough water or electricity here, and few found work. At first we lived on what we had saved, then we sold the women's gold, and now we sell our furniture day by day to live. We had a good life in our village; now we are beggars who depend on God and friends like Americans to help us." We sat on two long, narrow rugs, had tea, and watched his two boys play with toys he had carved from wood. They were small replicas of the agricultural tools of the area—a miniature shepherd's crook and an oxen yoke and plow. Outside in the courtyard his wife knotted a new rug for the house on an upright loom made of pipes and cotton threads. Not deterred by the hardships imposed by the two embargoes and bad economic conditions, she created a brightly colored carpet from bits of yarn that she had carefully extracted from discarded clothing and fabrics.

Next door an eighty-one-year-old Turkoman farmer originally from the village of Beersheer was weaving simple prayer rugs on a horizontal loom. His family had taken up the craft to survive. The Iraqi army had confiscated four thousand *dunums* (about 155 acres) of fertile land they had owned near Kirkuk and given them the choice of relocating to southern Iraq or Benaslawa. "There was no job farming here, so we began to weave prayer rugs. We had seen villagers weave, and we had to believe that we could learn," he told me.

Other families in Benaslawa were equally inventive in their fight to endure. One gathered stale bread from house to house to sell to herders, another kept a cow and made yogurt, a third repaired tires, and a fourth crocheted traditional Kurdish shoes. Most felt very fortunate to have survived. "We are lucky to have escaped. Our friends from the villages near Erbil ended up in a mass grave."

Migdad Ahmad, a young artist in Benaslawa showed us his monumental portrait of a well-loved Kurdish martyr Mama Risha; parliament had commissioned it for the government complex in Erbil. "But I don't create for money. I create for martyrs," he said. Blazing prominently in the left top corner of the canvas was Kurdistan's most important icon, Baba Gurgur, the gas flame at the oil fields at Kirkuk, adored by Kurds and prayed to by simple people as a god. The top right corner was adorned with a large red star, the symbol of martyrdom. "The martyrs of Kurdistan are many, as many as the stars in the sky, and they shine just as brightly for our cause."

Kak Ahmad and his family spent their days helping to rebuild the village called Bistana. In comparison to the cold cinder block *mujamma'a*, it was a warm, multi-hued adobe village that sat by a creek at the edge of a meadow next to a mountain. Most houses had corrals to the front or the side in which to keep a family's few sheep or goats at night. The men were shepherds, and the women made yogurt to sell, as well as cleaning and preparing food. They also shared in men's chores, and they were particularly proud of having participated in the building of their own houses, sometimes mixing adobe and other times building a wall or putting up a roof. Their interior decorating was inspired. Because they lacked wood, the women shaped their kitchen furniture and stoves from adobe. Their cabinets, counters, and even appliances often appeared to be folk sculptures growing right out of the mud walls.

After our visit in Bensalawa and Bistana, we drove to Erbil. Parliamentary deputies and governmental ministries there were dealing with tough problems. The Iraqi government's laying to waste of animals and cropland by chemical warfare and mines and the bombing, dynamiting, and bulldozing of millions of Kurdish homes and villages had taken a tragic toll on the infrastructure. Even so parliament had time to address philosophical needs; it had just passed a freedom of expression law. "Pencils and cameras saved our lives," said one member of parliament. In their fervor, the deputies also enacted a gun-control bill that would require men to turn their arms over to the government. One could but wonder how difficult it would be to disarm the private militia of the aghas and tribal chiefs.

Over dinner one night, Younis shared his story with me. He was frightened, genuinely worried about what he had learned about Iraq's biological weapons in the chemical corps. He was certain that the regime had the means to spread typhoid, cholera, influenza and dreadful man-made diseases and that it intended to use them. He knew of military leaders who had been executed for refusing to employ biological weapons during the Gulf War. The concerned chemical engineer corps was told that biological weapons were to be used only in Israel, never in Iraq, but Younis was not sure. There had been a recent outbreak of a disease near Chamchamal which Younis was certain was man-made. He assured me that it was very easy to infect a water source, such as the lake at Dukan Dam, and let the contamination flow downstream to its target. Younis was frightened, and he wanted desperately to leave the country.

Also, Younis was in love. The object of his affection was a beautiful, intelligent, educated Kurdish girl in London whom he wanted to marry, even though he had never met her. She was the cousin of his good friend Zana. "Zana says she is the perfect woman for me, and he has known her all of his life. When we are married, Zana and I will be like brothers." His words made me think of the ideas of my friend Leila.

My time in Kurdistan was growing short. I had come and gone several times since I first visited southeastern Turkey in May 1990. I knew that when I left this time I might not return for a long while. Over the past three years, the Kurds had become more than part of an intriguing culture or a humanitarian concern. They had become my friends.

Kurdistan was no longer an ancient land whose amorphous boundaries encompassed large pieces of five modern countries. It was the tea-houses on the Tigris and the "Turkish wedding tank" at Cizre, mines exploding in late afternoon fields and sweet mulberries at evening Ramadan picnics near Amadiya, shepherds taking their flocks to pasture across the old bridge and children crying "Hello Mister" in Zakho, women standing in the hot sun to vote and school children doing lessons by lamplight in Suleymaniye. I remembered the happiness of the weddings and births and the pain of the tragic endings. If I had learned one concrete lesson from my travels in Kurdistan it was the one Hero had predicted: to give each emotion its due and no more.

I remembered my first night in Iraqi Kurdistan, hovering on the side of a mountain at the Turkish border in April 1991. There had been little food, and everyone was sick. Yet Sherko and his family had invited me to stay in their tent and insisted on sharing their little food with me. The rain had been constant and death was all around us. That experience on the mountain had so marked me that I returned to northern Iraq two months later and entered the Safe-haven to look for my friends. Often people I met remembered me from the camp and that I had made the trek up the mountain many times bringing people water, blankets, and coats. Those small acts of kindness had opened an entire new world to me. But I had never found Sherko and his family and presumed that they were dead.

I took my time leaving, returning through Koisanjak to participate in mourning for Hameen Pawfeeq, the mother of my friend Dr. Atia Salihy. Hameen Khan had raised ten children, all doctors or Ph. D.'s, all active in the Kurdish cause. Presumably she had been killed to avenge the acts of her children. Atia was in London when the murder occurred and sent me back with money to have *xirobe*, a type of fried bread, prepared to distribute to the poor in her mother's honor. Still feeling the loss of Leila and Mr. Ali, I felt it appropriate that one of my last acts in Kurdistan was one that expressed bereavement.

I traveled to Amadiya and found the Sulaf Hotel inhabited by goats. A caretaker's family lived under the roof of a loading area in back of the hotel. Furniture was gone and windows broken in the once proud hotel from which I had fancied brave Kurdish warriors sallied forth. Posters with photographs of Mr. Ali and his murdered son described them as brave martyrs. For all of the housing problems in Kurdistan, no one had moved into the Sulaf Hotel. Down the road, clothes hung to dry between the marble columns of Saddam's former summer palace, and women knitted socks and did washing on the verandas of his lavish guest houses while young children played beside them.

I spent some of my last days in Kurdistan in Dahuk visiting friends, among them a young Yezidi woman, Adiba. As I showed her a small album I had made of my Kurdish experiences, my emotions went from happiness to sadness, from anger to contentment, just as they had on my journey. Adiba touched a photograph taken at the camp near Çukurca. "That's a wonderful photograph of Sherko. What terrible days those were."

"Sherko? You knew Sherko? What happened to him? When was the last time you saw him?"

"About twenty minutes ago. He left just before you arrived. He works with the reconstruction agency."

I felt like my heart had stopped beating. It was the same sensation that I had felt upon learning Aisha was alive after thinking that she was dead.

"How can I find him?"

Adiba picked up the telephone. About fifteen minutes later Sherko joined us. He greeted me with a big smile.

"Sherko!" I shrieked. "You are alive, well, and —look at you— even a little plump!"

He took me home to visit his family and insisted that we stay for dinner. In Çukurca we had shared Kurdish goat cheese, eggs, and tea; in Dahuk Sherko's wife piled on our plates serving after serving of stuffed vegetables, fresh Kurdish greens, and roasted chicken, a generous feast to celebrate our reunion. Alan, the baby born to her on the trek over the mountain had grown into an inquisitive toddler, and young Habib, who had followed me around the camp, was in first grade. Nine-year-old Diel managed a big smile as she served us tea.

Most of the Iraqi Kurds had survived, gone home, and begun to rebuild their villages. But their position was still precarious. They had a parliament and a de facto state, more than any other Kurds had obtained in this century, but many problems remained to be solved. After two years, I had found my friends alive and well, wanting to stay in Kurdistan, but poised to flee again if they must.

My odyssey was over. It was time for me to go home. I drove to Diyarbakir, flew to Istanbul and straight on to San Antonio. My first night there I attended the coronation of the Queen of The Order of the Alamo, a uniquely Texas pageant in which costumed debutantes chosen from prominent families are presented to society, each clad in sufficient finery to fund the rebuilding of several Kurdish villages. As the lights reflected the sparkle of the royals' sequins, I began to remember the sequined dresses in which Kurdish villagers had fled to the protection of the mountains near Çukurca and how sad they had looked in the persistent rain. The orchestra was playing a regal march but instead of debutantes, I saw exhausted women climbing to look for firewood and men carrying small dead babies covered with blankets. I could hear the children crying and feel the mud thick on my legs again. I could smell and almost touch the dead and dying who once more surrounded me. Rather than comforting, I found my homecoming painful.

As young Texas ladies paraded across an elegantly appointed stage and bowed to the audience, I thought of Leila's daughters at a similar age modeling their mother's legendary jewelry. As the placement of a crown on her head transformed my neighbor, a young Texas debutante, into Queen of the Court of Napoleonic Splendor, I thought of Hero and Kafiya, and how circumstances had transformed them from peshmerga into parliamentary deputy and Madame Minister. In brief hours I had traveled from one end of the spectrum to the other, and watching the Court of Napoleonic Splendor march out of San Antonio's auditorium and into waiting moving vans which would transport them to the next party, I wondered how I could exist in two such different worlds. I felt unsure of myself and nervous as I spoke with friends; my designer dress seemed to be a costume, and I found myself uncomfortable on what now seemed to be the wrong side of the camera, smiling for other photographers.

In the months ahead I would realize that I could never again be completely comfortable in either world. The pain of one would interfere with the pleasure of the other. My experiences in Kurdistan had intensified my sensibilities as a person born on a border, and I would grow ever closer to those who, like myself, cross boundaries and squarely face the challenge of living on both sides of lines that divide others.

Back in the comfort of my Texas home, I might forget the woes of my Kurdish friends and only remember stories of a feisty, beautiful mountain people, interesting, but not relevant to my life in Texas, their tragedies not my problem. But my friend Leila, no longer of this world, still enjoys visiting her friends and family in their dreams, and mine are no exception. In dreams Leila comes to me. We chat, laugh, and have tea together. We walk up the mountain to the spring at Sulaf and sit among the mulberry trees, where she takes my hand and says once more, "*Xisco men i*, you are my sister."

# GLOSSARY

*Agha*  A regional or tribal leader.

*Alevis*  Turkomans and Kurds who belong to a syncretic religion containing elements of Islam and older Turkish and Kurdish religions.

*Al-Anfal*  "The Spoils," a 1988 Iraqi military campaign designed to solve "the Kurdish problem," in which 50-100,000 Kurds were killed, many of them women and children.

*Aramaic*  A group of northwest Semitic languages spoken in Biblical times and still spoken by Jews and Christians from Kurdistan.

*Chaldean Catholics*  Former Nestorians who adopted the beliefs, but not the rituals or all of the practices, of the Roman Catholic Church, found mainly in northern Iraq.

*Elamites*  An ancient people who lived in what is now the Kurdish area, prophecies about whom some Christians think apply to present-day Kurds.

*Emirate*  An Ottoman province governed by an Emir. The Kurdish emirates included the Badinan, the Bhotan, the Soran, and the Baban.

*Jaash*  "Donkey foul," a derogatory term for the pro-Iraqi Kurdish militia.

*Jinn*  Spirits. Legend says Kurds descend from 500 *jinn* exiled from the Kingdom of Solomon and the 500 European virgins they took as brides to the Zagros mountains.

*Kak*  Kurdish for "brother," used by the peshmerga to address one another.

*Kalashnikov*  A Russian automatic attack weapon popular in Kurdistan.

*Khan*  A peculiarly Kurdish abbreviation for *khanum*, a title like "Lady."

*Kurmanji*  Kurdish dialect spoken in eastern Turkey and the Badinan district of Iraq.

*Medes*  An Iranian people who ruled parts of Iraq and Iran in the 9-6th centuries B.C. from whom the Kurds say they descend.

*Melek Taus*  The peacock angel who deals with this world according to the Yezidis.

*Naqshabandi*  A Sufi brotherhood important both spiritually and politically in Kurdistan.

*Newroz*  The March 21 Kurdish and Zoroastrian New Year celebrated by lighting fires.

*Peshmerga*  "Those who face death," Kurdish guerrilla fighters.

*Qu'ran*  (sometimes spelled Koran) The sacred scripture of Islam.

*Ramadan*  The Muslim month of fasting and prayer.

*Salah-al-din al-Ayyubi*  A Kurdish hero on whose bravery and generosity the code of chivalry is said to be based. Known in the West as Saladin, King of Jerusalem.

*Sheikh*  A title of respect for one in authority, particularly applied to religious leaders.

*Sheikh Adi*  The founder of the Yezidi religion and its most important saint.

*Sorani*  A Kurdish dialect spoken in the Soran and Baban areas of northern Iraq.

*Shi'ite*  "Partisans," a minority Moslem sect that believes Mohammed's cousin and son-in-law Ali should have followed him as leader of the Islamic communities.

*Sunni*  Followers of the traditional way or *sunnah* of Muslims.

*Treaty of Sevres*  The 1920 Treaty between Turkey and the allies that provided for the creation of an autonomous Kurdistan, superceded by the 1923 Treaty of Lausanne.

*Turkomans*  A broad collection of Turkic-speaking tribes located in Central Asia, northern Iraq and Iran, and parts of Turkey.

*Vilayet of Mosul*  An Ottoman province populated by Kurds, Turkomans, and Christians. It is now northern Iraq, although sometimes claimed by Turkey.

*Yezidis*  Followers of a religion peculiar to the Kurdish area.

*Zoroastrianism*  An Iranian religion which was prevalent in pre-Islamic Kurdistan. Based on the teachings of Zoroaster, it stresses the conflict between Good and Evil.

# SELECTED BIBLIOGRAPHY

Biggs, Robert D., editor. *Discoveries from Kurdish Looms*, Evanston: Northwestern University in conjunction with the Chicago Rug Society, 1983.

Bruinessen, M. van. *Agha, Shaikh and State: The Social and Political Structures of Kurdistan*, London and New Jersey: Zed Books, 1993.

Bulloch, J. and H. Morris. *No Friends but the Mountains: The Tragic History of the Kurds*, London: Penguin, 1993.

Cavanaugh, Lieutenant Colonel John P. *Operation Provide Comfort: A Model for Future NATO Operations*, Fort Leavenworth: School of Advanced Military Studies, United States Army Command and General Staff College, 1992.

Chaliand, G. *People without a Country: The Kurds and Kurdistan*, revised edition, Brooklyn: Olive Branch Press, 1993.

Committee to Protect Journalists. *Enforced Restraint: Press Conditions in Turkey*, New York, 1990.

Eagleton, W. *The Kurdish Republic of 1946*, London: Oxford University Press, 1963.

———. *An Introduction to Kurdish Rugs and Other Weaving*, Buckhurst Hill, England, Scorpion Publishing Ltd, 1988.

Edmonds, C.J. *Kurds, Turks, and Arabs: Politics, Travel, and Research in North-Eastern Iraq, 1919-1925*, London: Oxford University Press, 1957.

Entessar, Nader. *Kurdish Ethnonationalism*, Boulder and London: Lynne Rienner Publishers, 1992.

Glassemlou, A. R., *Kurdistan and the Kurds*, Prague: Czech Academy of Sciences, 1965.

Guest, J.S. *Survival Among the Kurds: A History of the Yezidis*, London: KPI, 1993.

Gunter, M.M. *The Kurds in Turkey: A Political Dilemma*, Boulder: Westview Press, 1990.

———. *The Kurds of Iraq: Tragedy and Hope*, New York: St. Martin's Press, 1992.

Hamilton, A. M. *Road Through Kurdistan: An Engineer in Iraq*, London: Faber and Faber, 1937.

Helsinki Watch, A Division of Human Rights Watch. *The Kurds of Turkey: Killings, Disappearances and Torture*, New York, 1993.

Hansen, H. H. *Daughters of Allah: Among Muslim Women in Kurdistan*, London: George Allen and Unwin, 1960.

———. *The Kurdish Woman's Life: Field Research in Muslim Society, Iraq*, Copenhagen: National Museum, 1961.

Hitchens, C. (photographer E Kashi.) "Struggle of the Kurds," National Geographic, Vol. 182, No. 2, August 1992.

Human Rights Foundation of Turkey. *Turkey Human Rights Report 1991*, Ankara, 1992.

———. *Turkey Human Rights Report 1992*, Ankara, 1993.

———. *Turkey Human Rights Report 1993*, Ankara, 1994.

Ismet, I. G. *The PKK: A Report on Separatist Violence in Turkey, 1973-1992*, Ankara: Turkish Daily News Publications, 1992.

Izady, M. *The Kurds: A Concise Handbook*, Washington, Philadelphia, London: Taylor and Francis International Publishers, 1992.

Kahn, M. *Children of the Jinn: In Search of the Kurds and their Country*, New York: Seaview Books, 1981.

Kashi, E. (photographer), Hitchens, C. (introduction). *When the Borders Bleed*, New York: Pantheon Books, 1994.

Kasraian, N. (photographer), Arshi, Z. and Zabihi, K., (text). *Kurdistan*, Ostersund: Oriental Art Publishing, 1990.

Kreyenbroek, P.G. and S. Sperl, editors. *The Kurds: a Contemporary Overview*, London: Routledge, 1992.

Kreyenbroek, P. G. *Yezidism: Its Background, Observances, and Textual Traditions*, Lewiston: Edwin Mellen Press, 1995.

The Kurdish Library. *The International Journal of Kurdish Studies* (formerly *The Kurdish Times*), New York, 1989-1994.

Laber, J. "The Hidden War in Turkey," New York Review of Books, Vol. 41, No. 12, June 23, 1994.

Laizer, S. *Into Kurdistan: Frontiers Under Fire*, London and New Jersey: Zed Books Ltd., 1991.

Layard, A. H. *Discoveries in the Ruins of Ninevah and Babylon with Travels in Armenia, Kurdistan and the Desert*, London: John Murray, 1853.

Makiya, K. "The Anfal: Uncovering an Iraqi Campaign to Exterminate the Kurds," *Harper's*, May 1992.

McDowall, D. *The Kurds: A Nation Denied*, London: Minority Rights Publications, 1992.

Meadowcroft, M. and M. Lunn. "Kurdistan: Monitoring Report, Elections for Iraqi National Assembly and Leader of the Kurdistan Liberation Movement," Electoral Reform Society Services, London, 1992.

Middle East Watch, A Division of Human Rights Watch. *Genocide in Iraq: The Anfal Campaign Against the Kurds*, New York, London, 1993.

Miller, J. (photographer, S. Meiselas) "Iraq Accused: A Case of Genocide," *New York Times Magazine*, January 3, 1993.

Olson, R. *The Emergence of Kurdish Nationalism and the Sheikh Said Rebellion*, 1920-1925, Austin: University of Texas Press, 1977.

Omaran, Y. "Turkish Journalists Pressured from All Sides," *Attacks on the Press in 1993*, New York: Committee to Protect Journalists, 1994.

O'Shea, M. "Greater Kurdistan, Towards a More Realistic Approach?" Masters Thesis, School of Oriental and African Studies, London University, 1992.

Sabar, Y. *The Folk Literature of the Kurdistani Jews: an Anthology*, Yale Judaica Series, Vol. XXIII, New Haven and London: Yale University Press, 1982.

Schmidt, Dana Adams. *Journey Among Brave Men*, Boston: Little Brown and Co., 1964.

Soane, E. B., *Through Mesopotamia and Kurdistan in Disguise*, London: John Murray, 1912.

Stanzer, W. *Kordi: Lives, Rugs, Flatweaves of the Kurds in Khorasan*, Vienna, 1988.

Whitman, L., *Destroying Ethnic Identity: The Kurds of Turkey, an Update*, New York: Helsinki Watch, 1990.

# Photographs

Destruction and Rebuilding

1. Iraqi Kurds crossing the Little Zab during flight to Turkey, April 1991.
2. Camp of Iraqi Kurds on Turkish border, near the village of Çukurca, Turkey, April 1991.
3. Funeral at Iraqi-Kurdish camp, near Çukurca, Turkey, April 1991.
4. Iraqi Kurdish boy reaching for bread from relief truck, camp near Çukurca, Turkey, April 1991.
5. Kurds trying to light fire at camp near Çukurca, Turkey, April 1991.
6-7. Displaced Kurds returning to houses in destroyed town of Qala Diza, Iraq, July 1991.
8. Displaced children from Kirkuk area living at former Iraqi Security Building, Suleymaniye, Iraq, March 1993.
9. Water distribution rack with taps, camp for displaced Kurds at former Iraqi Security Building, Suleymaniye, Iraq, March 1993.
10. Kurdish girl displaced from Kirkuk area, camp at former Iraqi Security Building, Suleymaniye, Iraq, March 1993.
11. Kurdish woman displaced from Kirkuk area weaving rug with salvaged yarn, concentration village of Benaslawa, Iraq, April 1993.
12. Kurdish school girl displaced from Kirkuk area with book bag made by her mother, Lana School, concentration village of Benaslawa, Iraq, April 1993.
13. Recess at school damaged by Iraqi troops, Penjwin, Iraq, December 1992.
14. Studying in cold school building, Penjwin, December 1992.

Iraqi Kurdistan

15. Peshmerga by waterfall at Sulaf, Iraq, May 1991.
16. Woman walking to head spring at Sulaf, Iraq, May 1991.
17. Muslim woman reading Qu'ran as part of private Ramadan observance, Sulaf, Iraq, June 1991.
18. Ottoman Bridge at Zakho, Iraq, March 1993.
19. Kurdish agricultural worker harvesting grain by traditional methods, near Dahuk, Iraq, July 1991.
20. Kurdish shepherd taking flock to pasture, Zakho, Iraq, March 1993.
21. Kurdish shepherds' camp near ruins of old Christian church, Zakho, Iraq, March 1993.
22. Dahuk, Iraq, December 1992.
23. Suleymaniye, Iraq, March 1993.
24. Young women at commemoration of 1991 Kurdish uprising, Suleymaniye, Iraq, March 1993.
25. Peshmerga selling first spring flowers, Suleymaniye, Iraq, March 1993.
26. Kurdish village girl picking flowers near Rowanduz, Iraq, April 1993.

Kurdish Election

27. Sign at Habur Bridge across Tigris River entering Kurdish Iraq, May 1992.
28. Kurdish men campaigning for Massoud Barzani, near Zakho, May 1992.
29. Kurdish family campaigning for Massoud Barzani, Dahuk, Iraq, May 1992.

30. Kurdish women voters bringing cakes and flowers to election officials, Suleymaniye, Iraq, May 1992.
31. Kurdish woman voting with election official Fatma Ahmad looking on, Suleymaniye, May 1992.
32. Jalal Talabani inking finger to vote in Kurdish elections, Qala Chwalan, May 1992.
33. Kurdish woman showing inked finger to prove that she has voted, Suleymaniye, May 1992.

DEFORESTATION
34. Kurdish woman carrying wood past a cemetery, the Badinan countryside, Iraq, December 1992.
35. Kurdish women resting after wood gathering, the Soran countryside, Iraq, December 1992.
36. Kurds chopping wood, Soran area, Iraq, December 1992.
37. Kurdish girl carrying wood, Soran area, December 1992.
38. Cemetery, last safe place for trees, Soran area, Iraq, December 1992.
39. "Forest for sale," Erbil, Iraq, October 1992.

ZHINAN: THE WOMEN OF KURDISTAN
40. Women preparing *Xirobe*, a type of fried bread to distribute to mourners, Koisanjak, Iraq, March 1993.
41-42. Weavers at home in Van, Turkey, April 1993.
43-44. Barzani women, Qush Tape, March 1993.
45. Woman building roof for her house, the Badinan, Iraq, December 1992.
46. Kurdish woman washing at Saddam's former summer palace, the Badinan region, Iraq, March 1993.
47. Kurdish woman preparing food at rebuilt village near Erbil, Iraq, April 1993.
48. Kurdish woman in sheep corral of house she helped rebuild, village near Erbil, Iraq, April 1993.

PESHMERGA
49. Mud stove and oven at peshmerga camp near Penjwin, Iraq, July 1991.
50. Jalal Talabani, founder of Patriotic Union of Kurdistan, Sulaf Hotel, Sulaf, Iraq, June 1991.
51. "Mam Rustum" Rustum Mohammed Rahim, peshmerga leader, Qala Chwalan, Iraq, July 1991.
52. Iranian Kurd bids her peshmerga sister goodbye, in mountains on Iraq-Iran border, July 1991.
53. Hero Talabani, Shaqlawa, Iraq, July 1991.
54. Peshmerga baking, camp near Penjwin, Iraq, July 1991.
55. Bekir Haji Safir, peshmerga camp near Penjwin, Iraq, July 1991.
56. Ibrahim Ahmad, Qala Chwalan, Iraq, July 1991.
57. Grave of peshmerga martyr, Koisanjak, Iraq, December 1992.

KURDISH TURKEY
58. Portrait of Turkish Kurd, southeastern Turkey, May 1990.
59. Traditional Kurdish mud house with irrigation ditch, Van, Turkey, May 1990.
60. Traditional Kurdish house interior, Van, Turkey, April 1993.
61. Young Kurdish man plowing, near Bitlis, Turkey, April 1993.
62. Kurdish woman preparing corn, near Sirnak, Turkey, April 1993.
63. Kurdish boys shining shoes, Batman, Turkey, February 1993.
64. School children returning home, Sirnak, Turkey, February 1993.
65. Children living in artillery battered home, Sirnak, Turkey, February 1993.

66. Standoff between Turkish soldiers and Kurdish women, Cizre, Turkey, March 1993.
67. Kurdish girl in front of home repaired with vegetable oil cans, Cizre, Turkey, March 1993.

KURDISH HANDICRAFTS

68. Turkoman weaver, concentration village of Benaslawa, Iraq, April 1993.
69-70. Kurdish women displaced from Kirkuk area by making grain storage pots at former Iraqi Security building, Suleymaniye, Iraq, October 1992.
71. Matriarch of Christian weaving family spinning, Dahuk, Iraq, April 1993.
72. Daughter in-law of spinner putting last touches on traditional Badinani or "Christian" suit, Dahuk, April 1993.

CELEBRATION AND MOURNING

73. Remains of Jewish synagogue, Zakho, Iraq, September 1992.
74. Drummer awakens Islamic faithful for early breakfast before beginning a day of fasting during Ramadan, Zakho, Iraq, March 1993.
75. Yezidi procession at Feast of the Assembly at the holy city of the Yezidis, Lalish, Iraq, September 1992.
76. Plaits of hair put on Yezidi grave as part of ritual mourning, near Dahuk, Iraq, March 1992.
77. Tomb of Sheikh Adi, Lalish, Iraq, September 1992.
78. Sanctuary of Sheikh Adi, Lalish, Iraq, September 1992.
79. Kurdish Muslim women visiting the grave of a young man the third day after he was killed, Rawanduz, Iraq, April 1993.
80. Shiite woman mourning for deaths of their martyrs Ali and Hussein, Aralik, Turkey, August 1990.
81-82. Fires on the eve of *Newroz*, Cizre, Turkey, March 1993.
83. Young man gives victory sign for Kurdish cause through flaming tires which will become a *Newroz* fire, Cizre, Turkey, March 1993.

*"Kurdistan and the villages will not be destroyed;
The Kurds cannot be stopped easily."*

Ibrahim Ahmad
Balik, Iraq
July 1991

2

5

8

9

II

12

*"We hope when our tragedy is over
that you will visit us in Kurdistan,
climb our mountains and sit by our waterfalls,
eat our tasty fruit and drink our sweet water."*

Sherko
Kurdish camp at Iraq's Border with Turkey
April 1991

15

19

21

23

*"We must take hold of our own affairs
and move forward;
we cannot be viewed as pathetic refugees forever.
A political, not a humanitarian,
solution is needed for our problems."*

Fatma Ahmad
A Woman election official
Suleymaniye, Iraq
May 1992

29

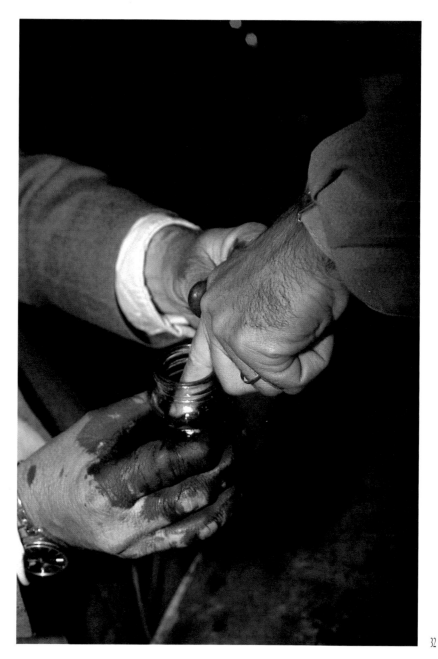

*"The forests of Kurdistan are destroyed.
People are even taking the tree roots for fuel.
With the root system gone,
the thin topsoil will wash away with the spring rains.
The United Nation's hesitation in shipping fuel here
is provoking an ecological disaster."*

Dr. Sait Ketani, forest expert
Salahaddin, Iraq
October 1992

38

39

"Xisco men i, *You are my sister.*"

Leila, wife of Ali Sheban
Amadiya, Iraq
June 1991

41

45

*"Men and women fight side by side in the mountains.*
*We fight so that our children will live safely in a free Kurdistan.*
*All of us are peshmerga;*
*all of us face death for Kurdistan."*

Kafiya, wife of Haji Bekir Safir
Penjwin, Iraq
July 1991

53

54

56

*"When Prime Minister Demirel says,*
*'The patience of the Turkish people is running out,'*
*he is sending a clear signal to those on the right*
*that they will have a free reign to kill Kurds."*

Haşim Haşimi
Mayor of Cizre, Turkey
March 1993

58

*"There was no job for us farming here,
so we began to weave prayer rugs.
We had seen villagers weave,
and we had to believe that we could learn."*

Turkoman weaver displaced from Kirkuk area
Concentration village of Benaslawa, Iraq
April 1993

69

*"Almost every Kurd has lost*
*a close family member recently,*
*yet we continue to dance and sing and celebrate life.*
*That's part of the strength of the Kurds.*
*We give each emotion its due and no more.*
*If we were to give too much time to happiness,*
*too much to sadness, we would go quite mad."*

Hero Talabani
Kalachwalan, Iraq
July 1992

74

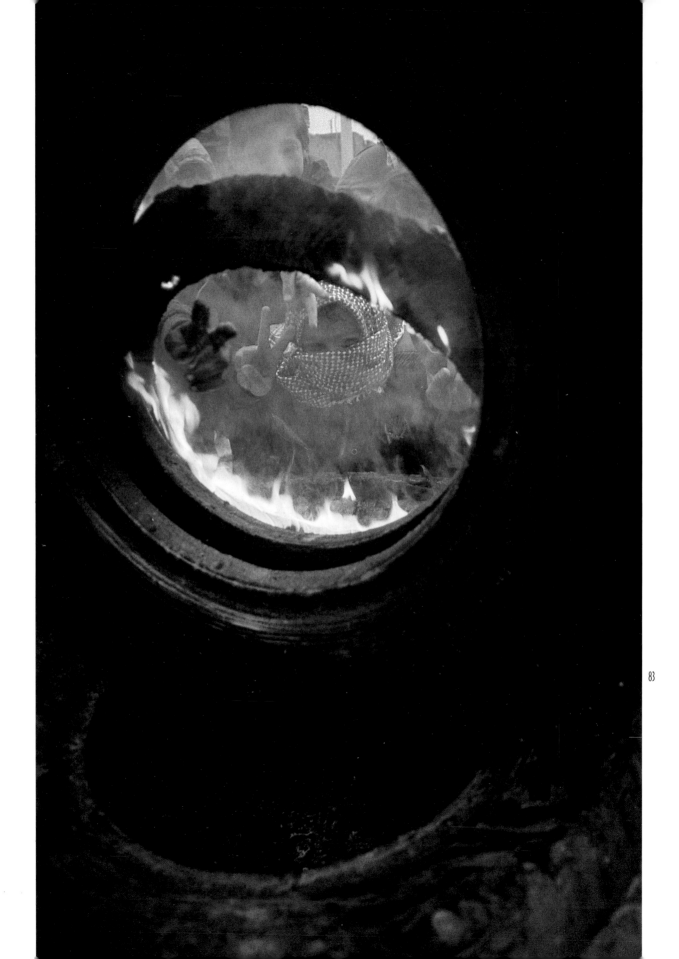